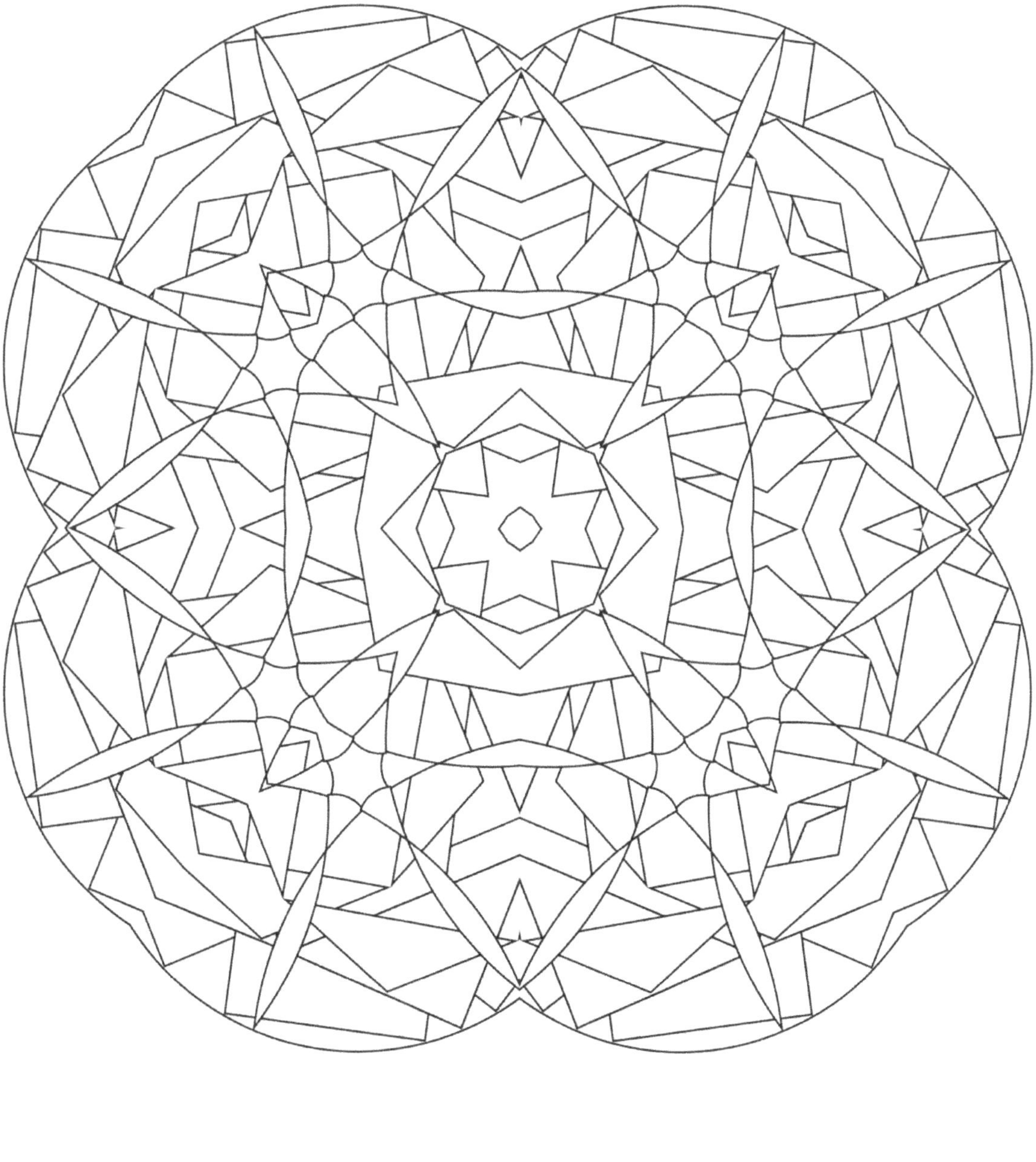

COLORING

IS A PERFECT WAY TO

RELAX, ESCAPE

AND

CREATE

This book was created

for

adults and children.

Welcome to Book One of the
<u>KALIDESCOPE SERIES</u>

Get out your markers, colored pencils, gel pens, or watercolor pencils and begin a wonderous journey coloring kalidescopes!

A blank piece of paper has been intentionally placed between each kalidescope. However, you might want to place another sheet of paper or thin cardboard behind the design before you begin to color. This will catch any bleed through colors and provide a place for you to make notes if you wish. I find sometimes that I need to write down the color and it's number that I used in case I want to use it again.

Feel free to make copies of the page before you color in case you want to color the same design again or share with friends at parties or get togethers.

Every master piece you create will look different!

Enjoy!

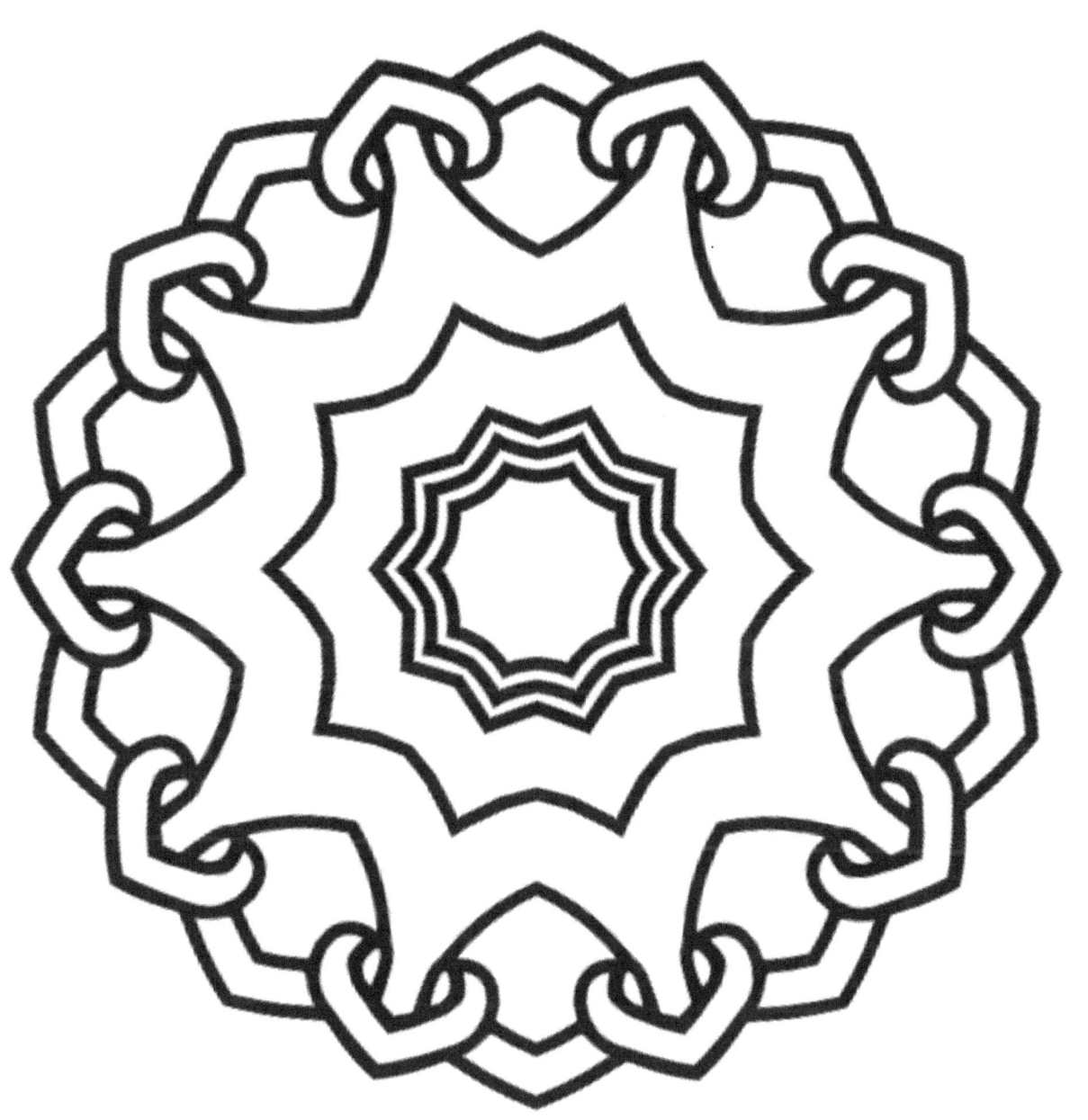

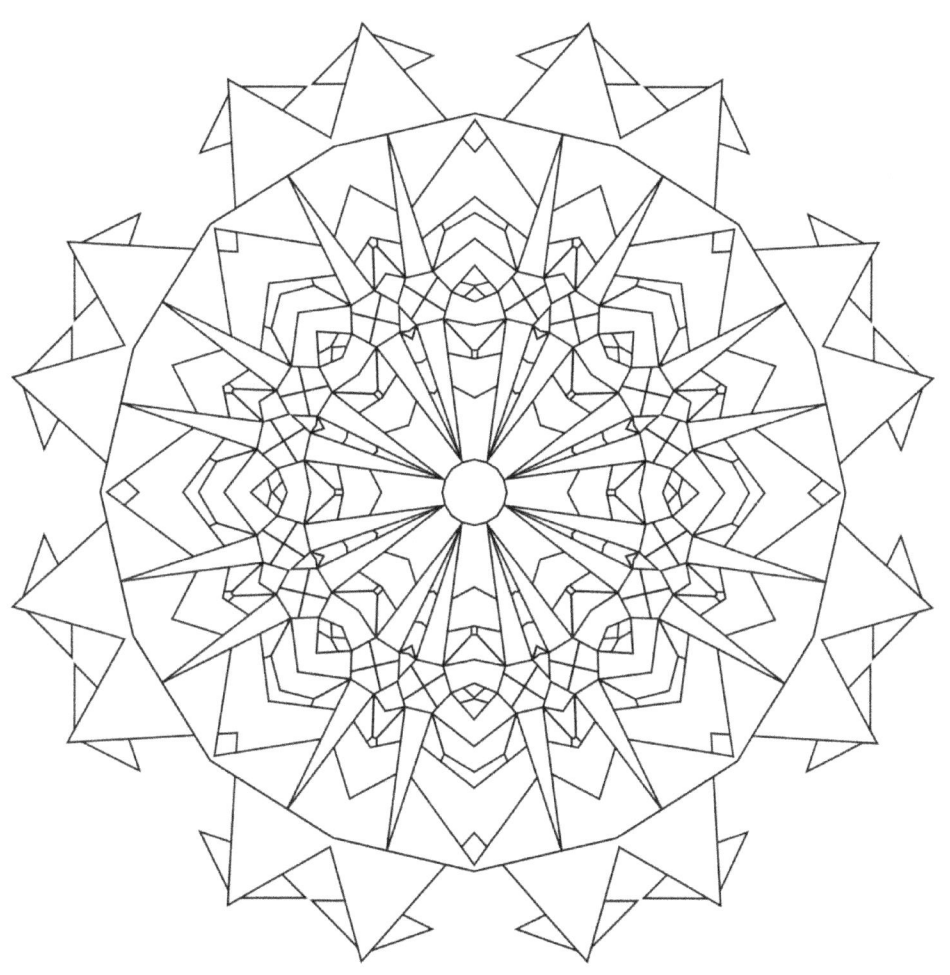

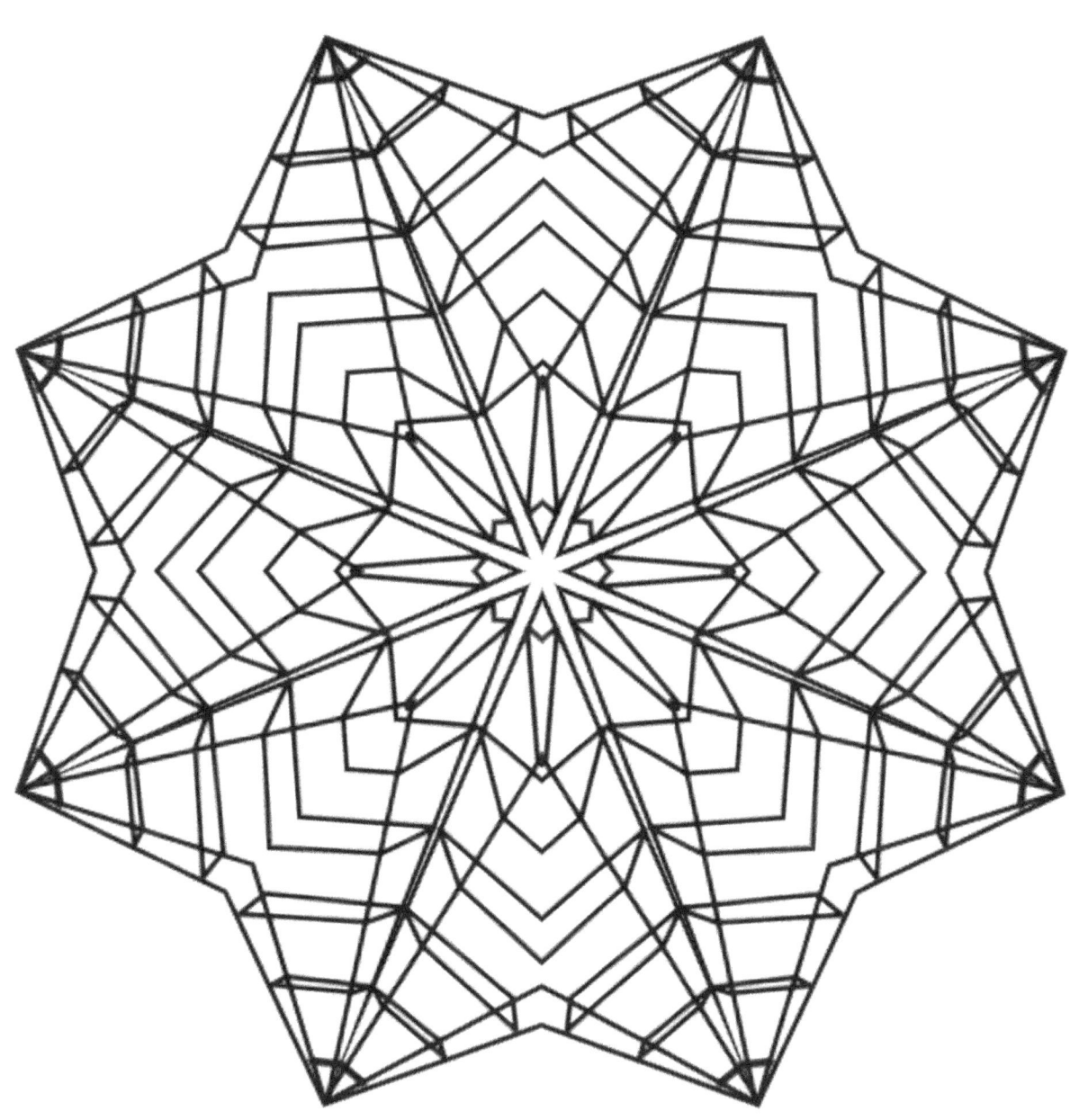

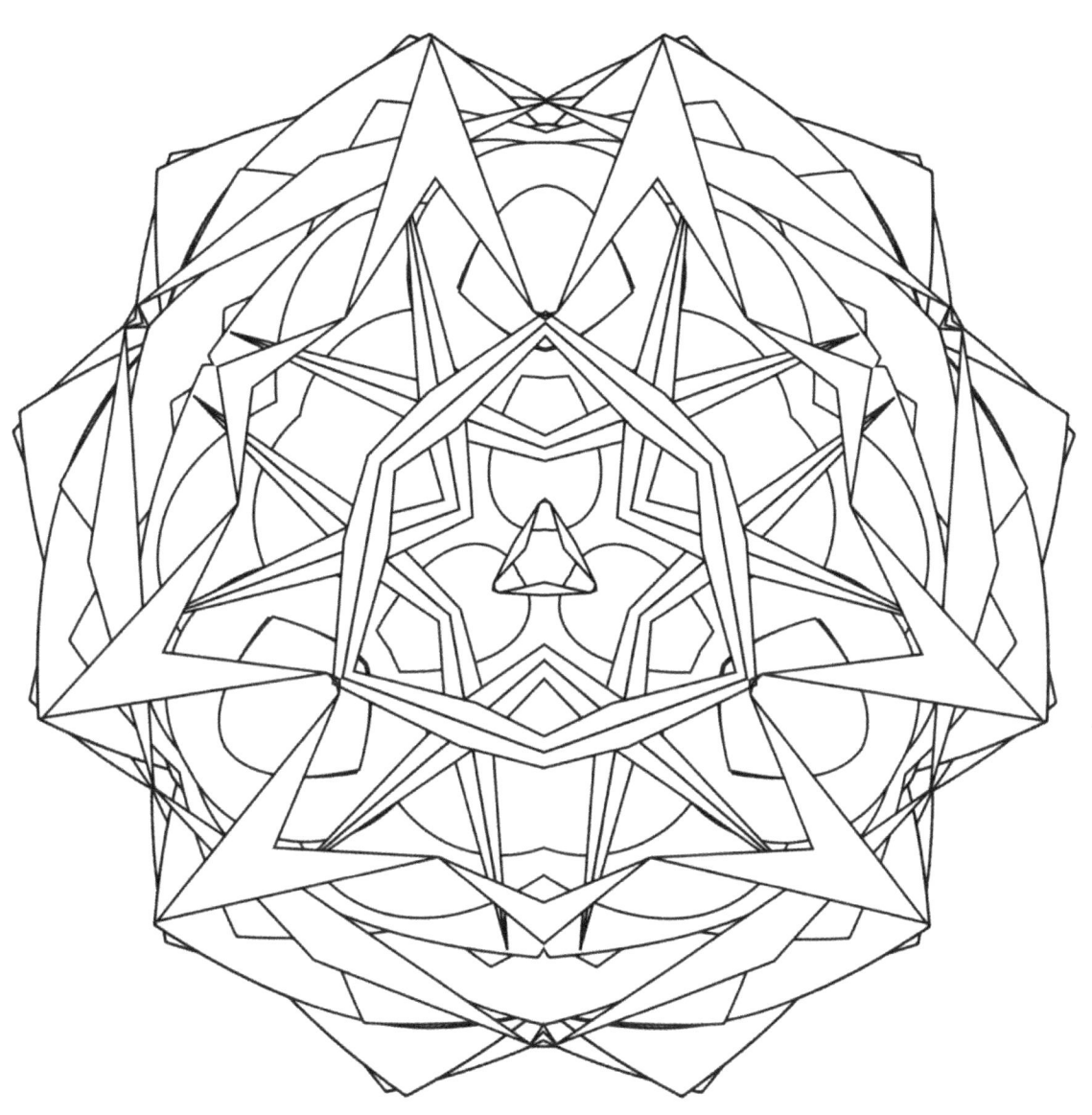

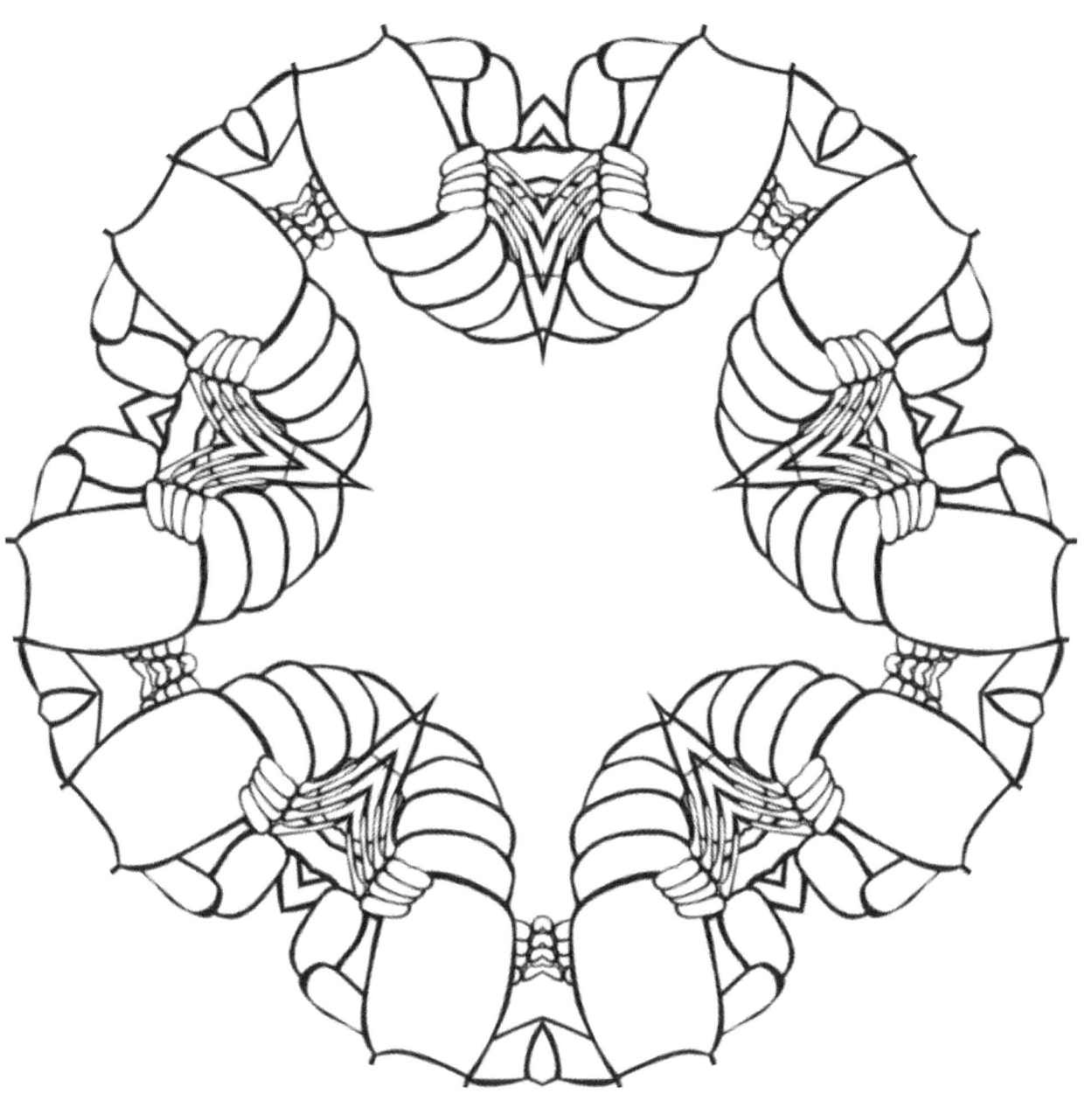

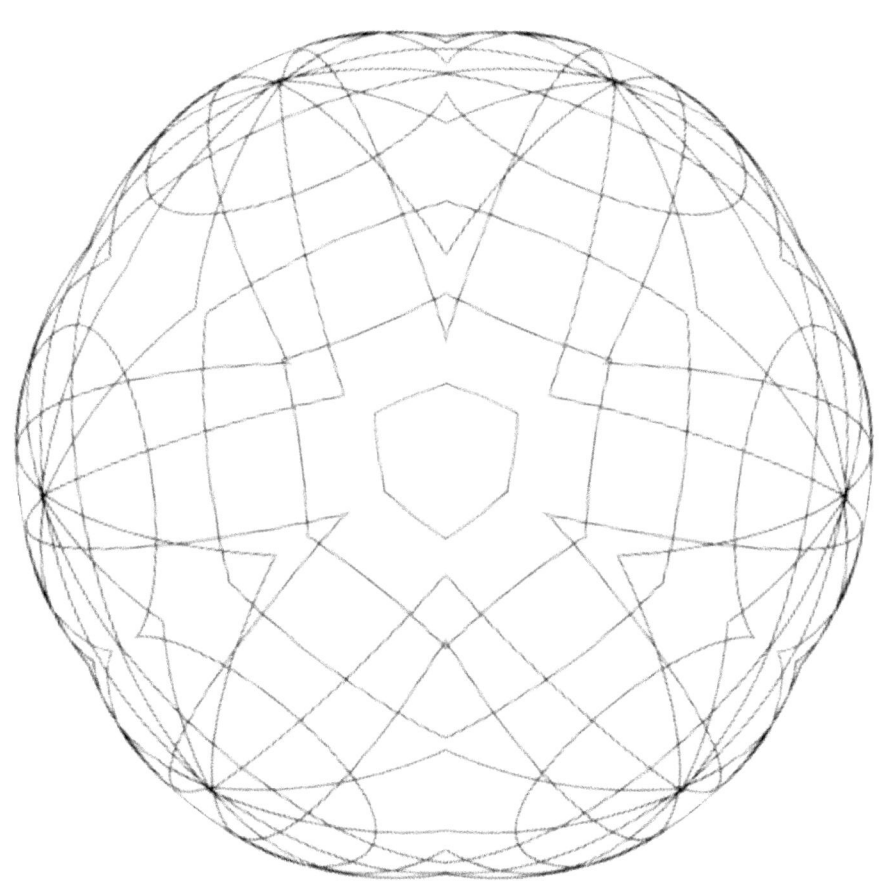

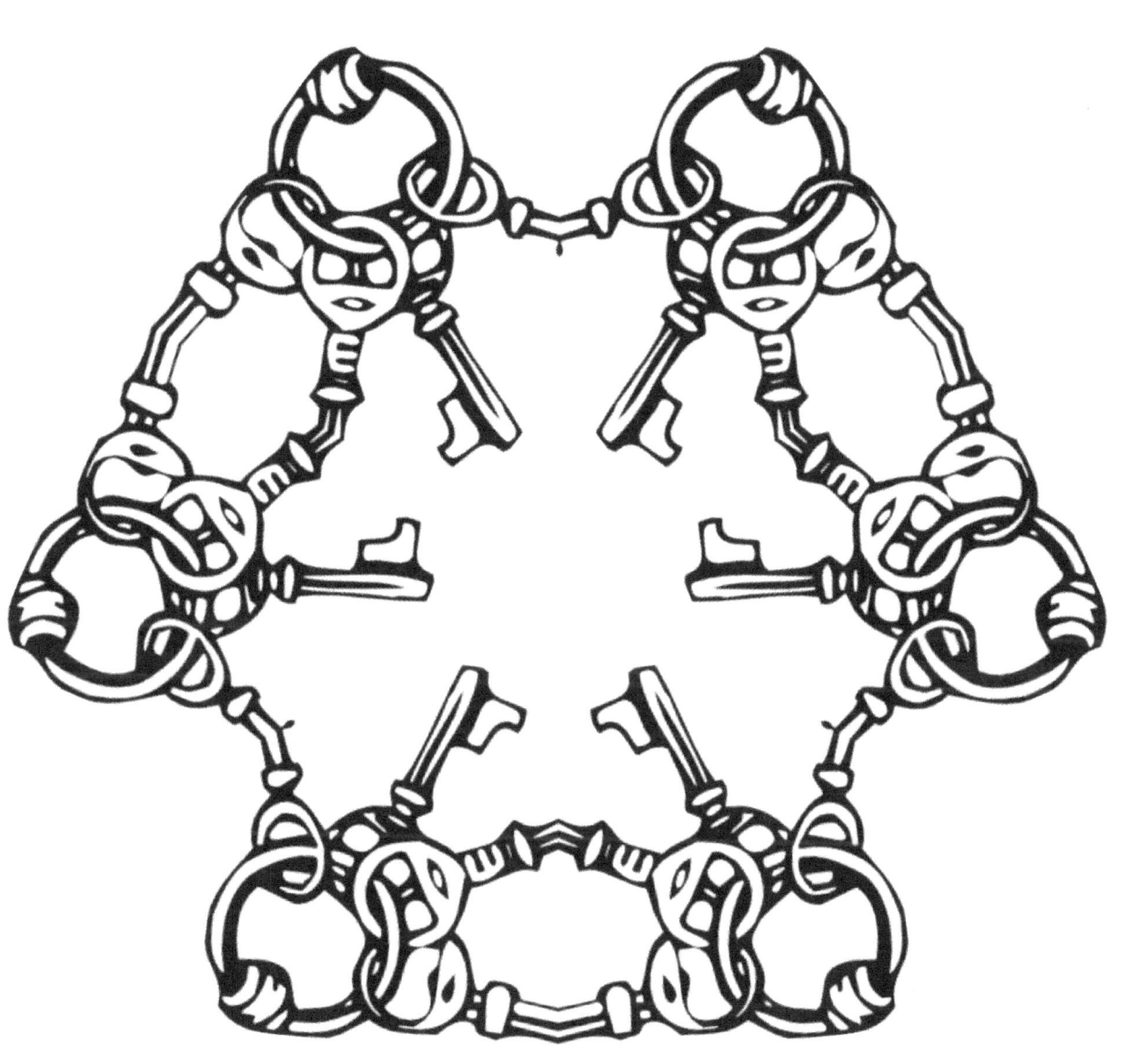

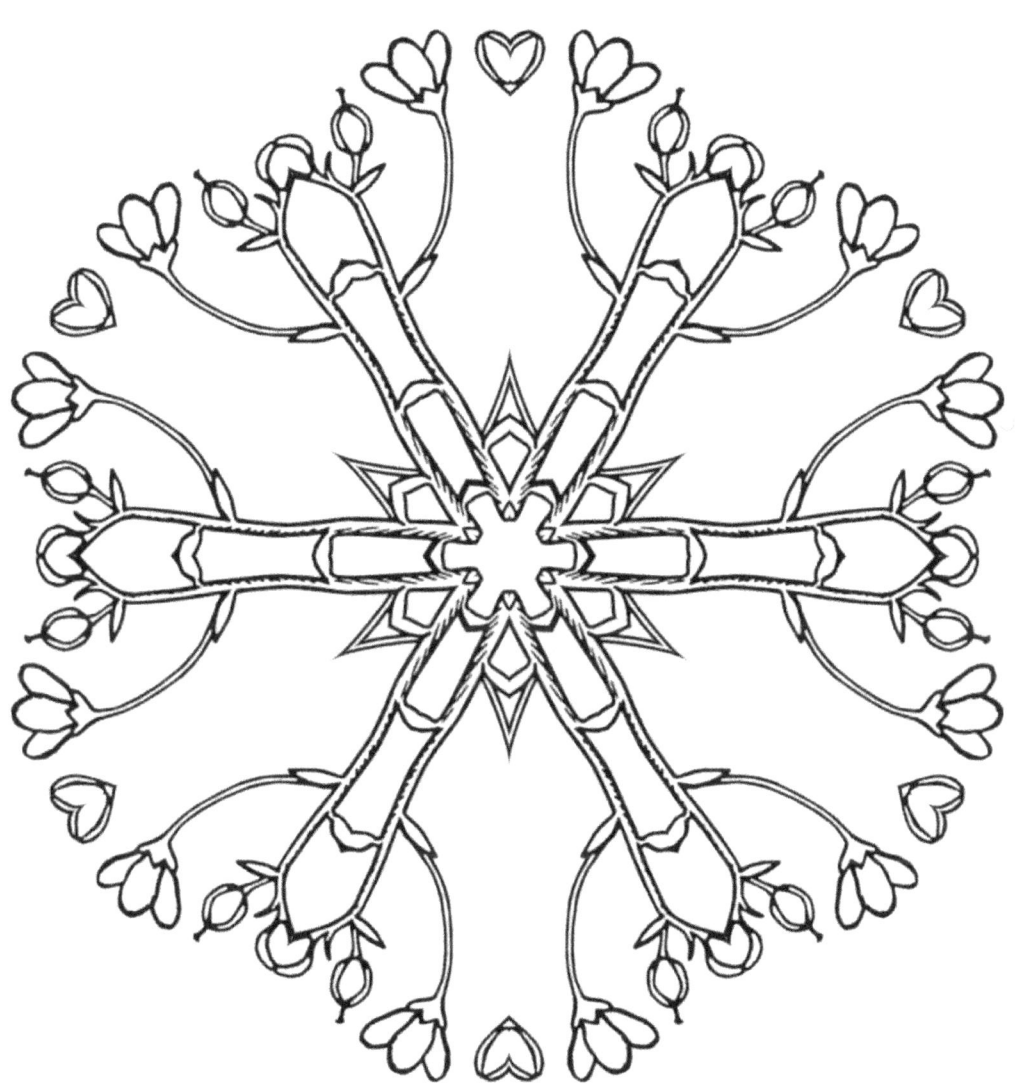

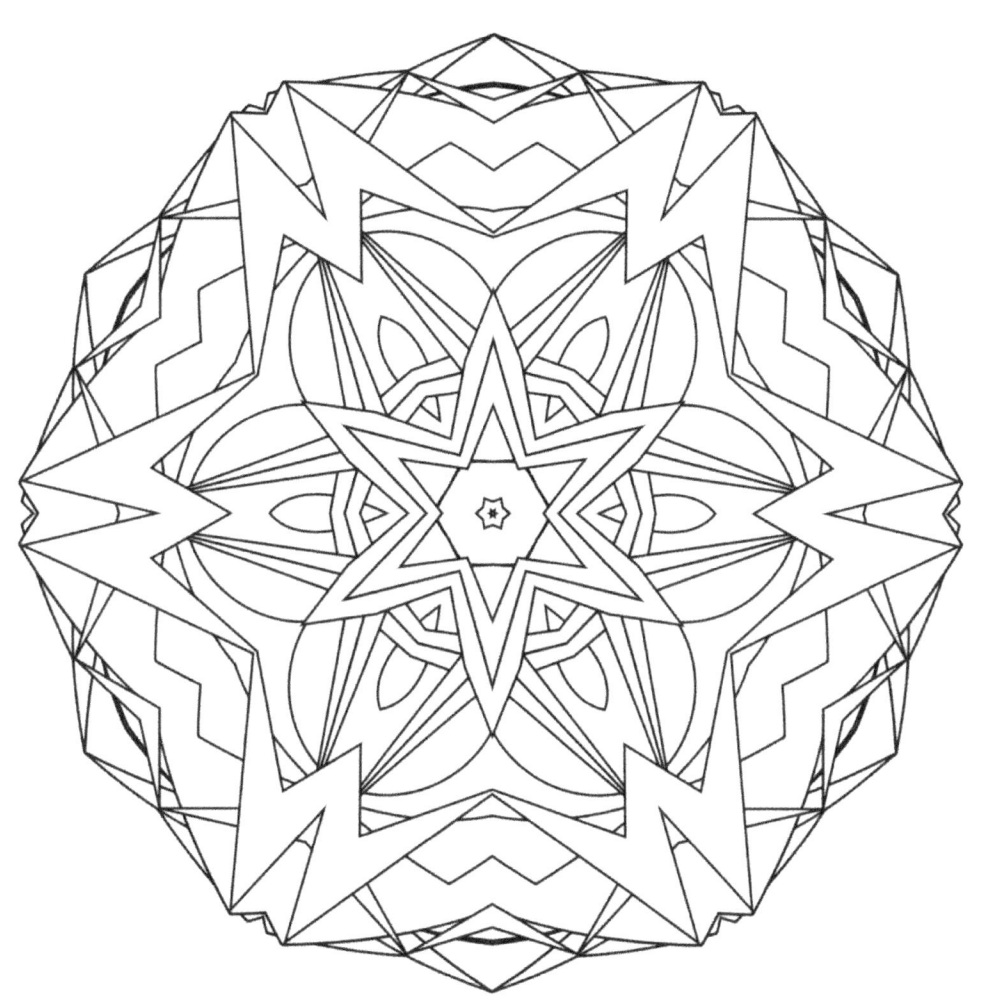

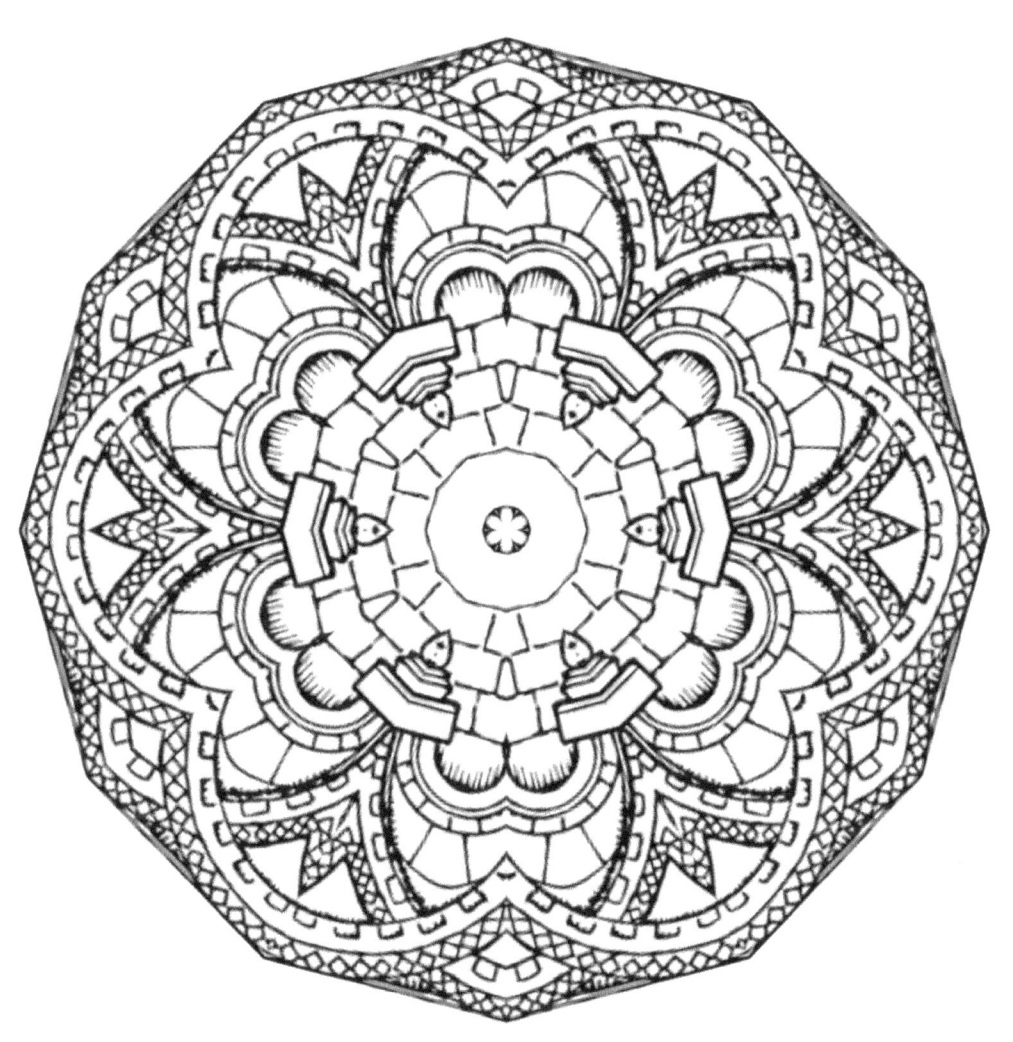

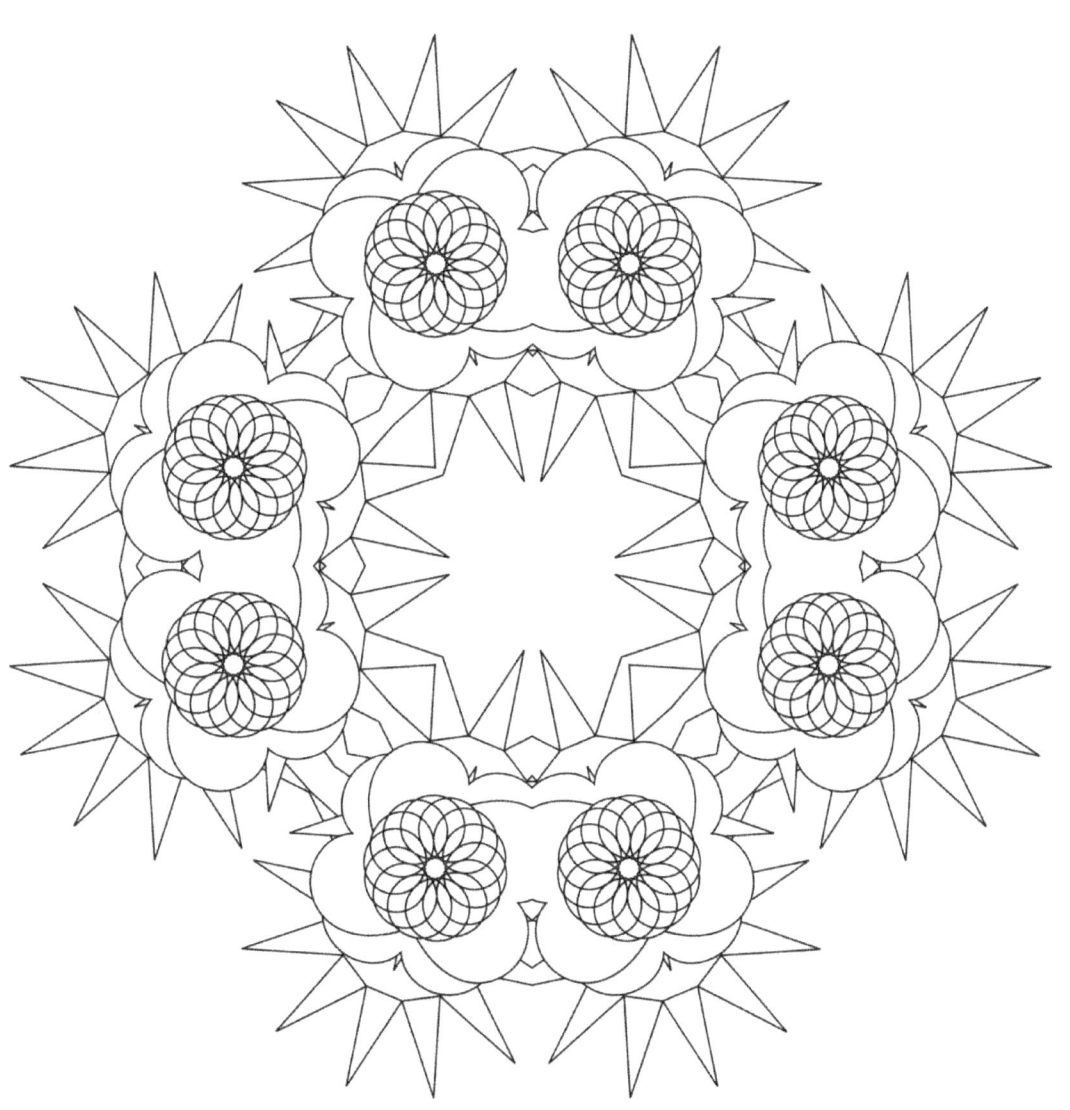

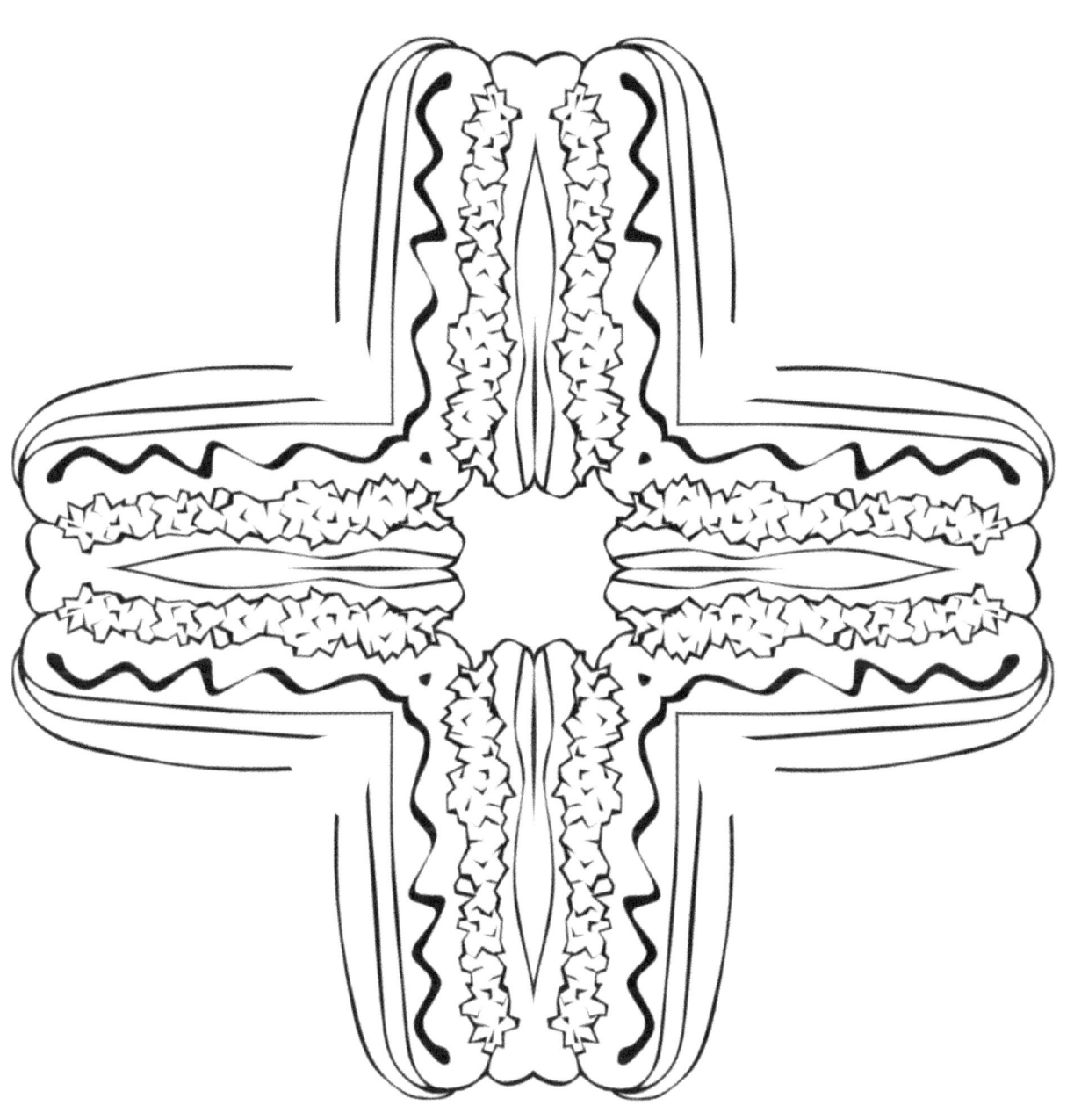

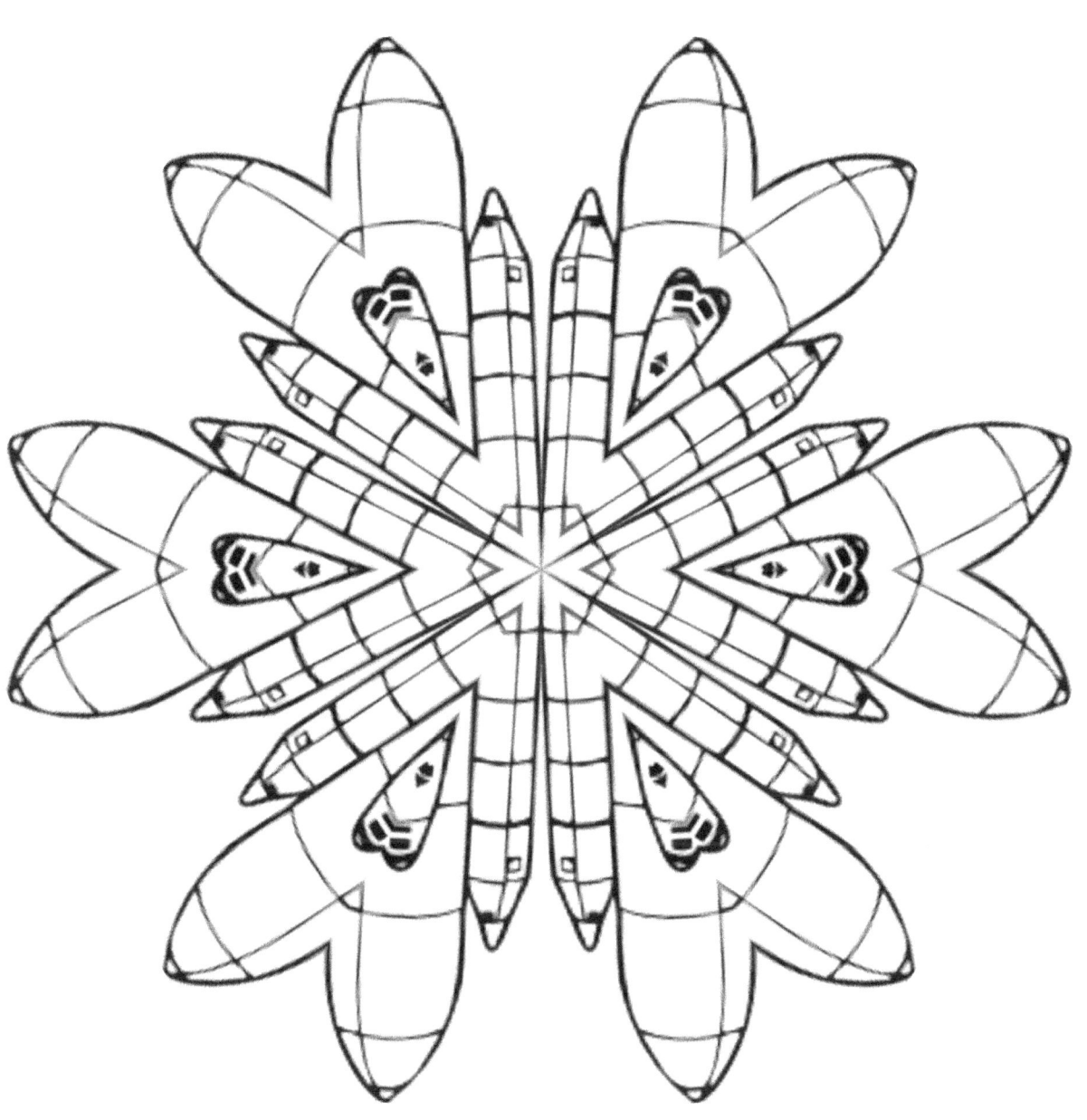

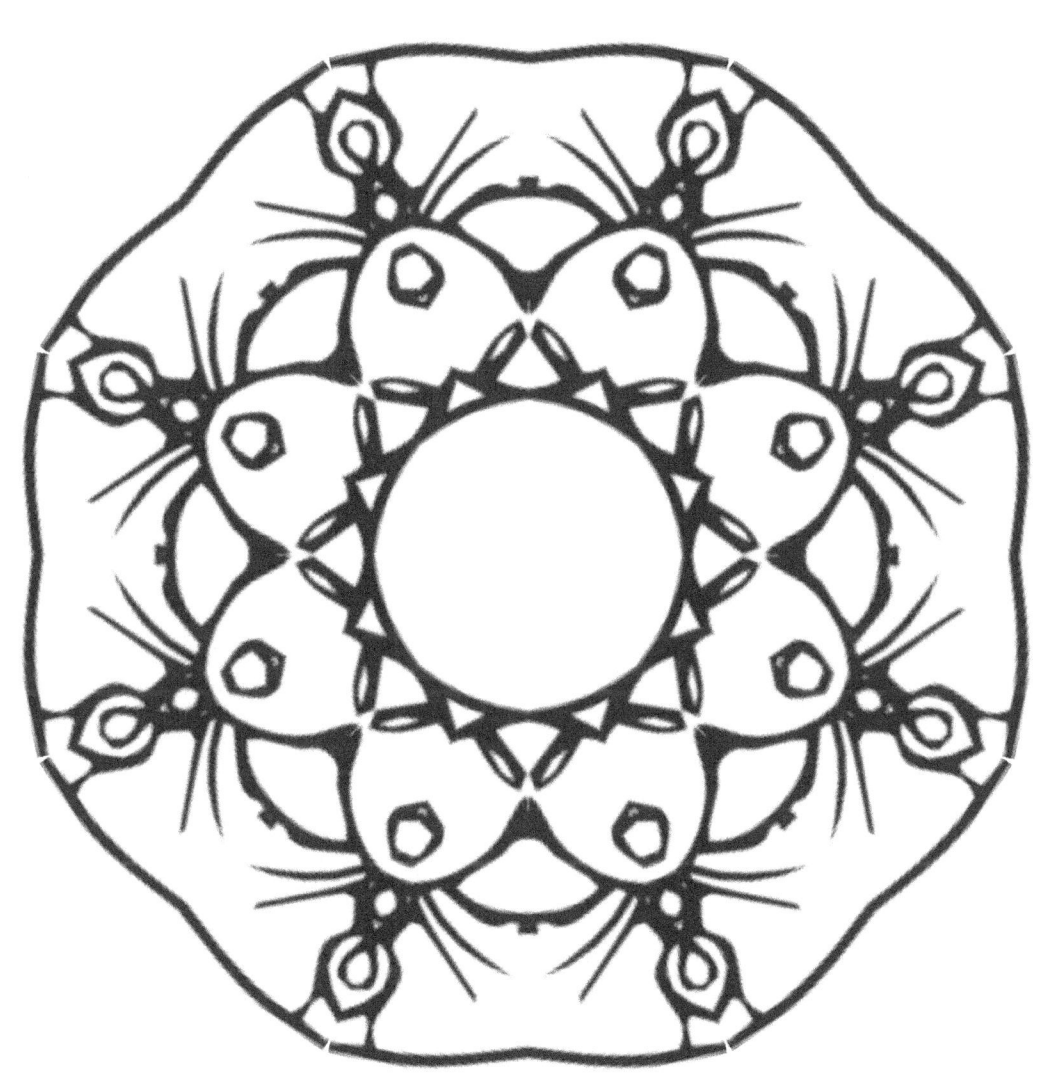

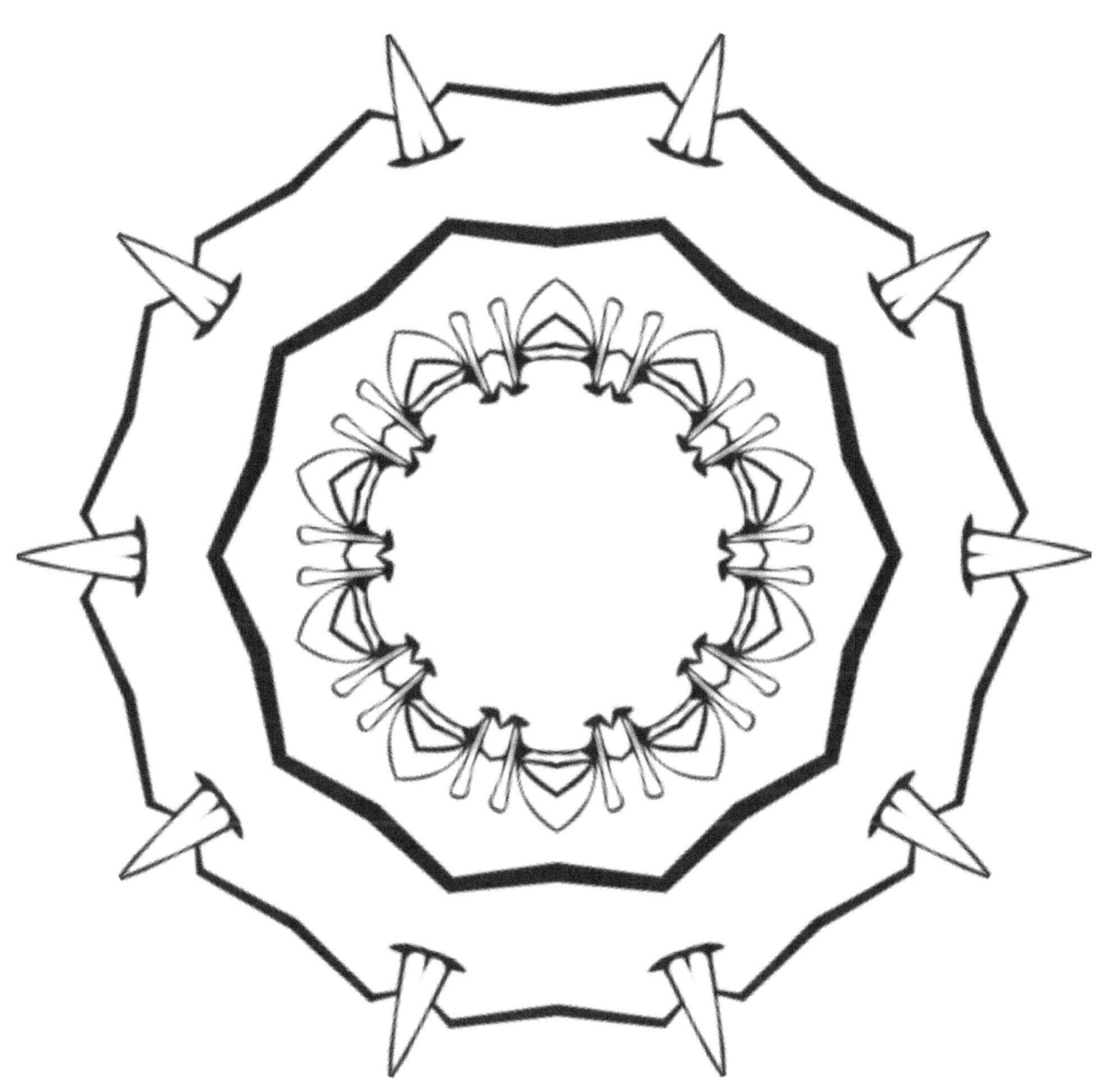

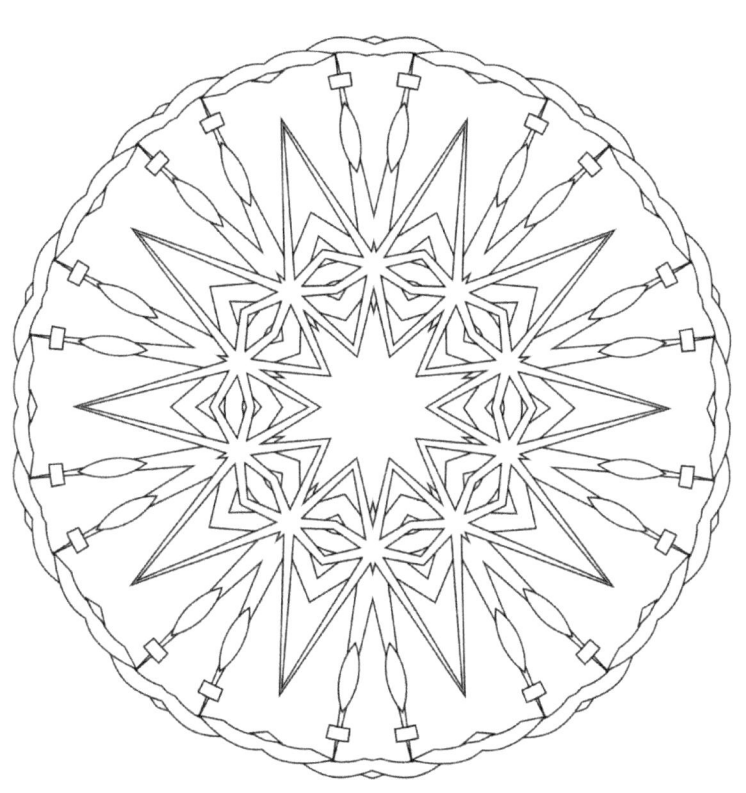

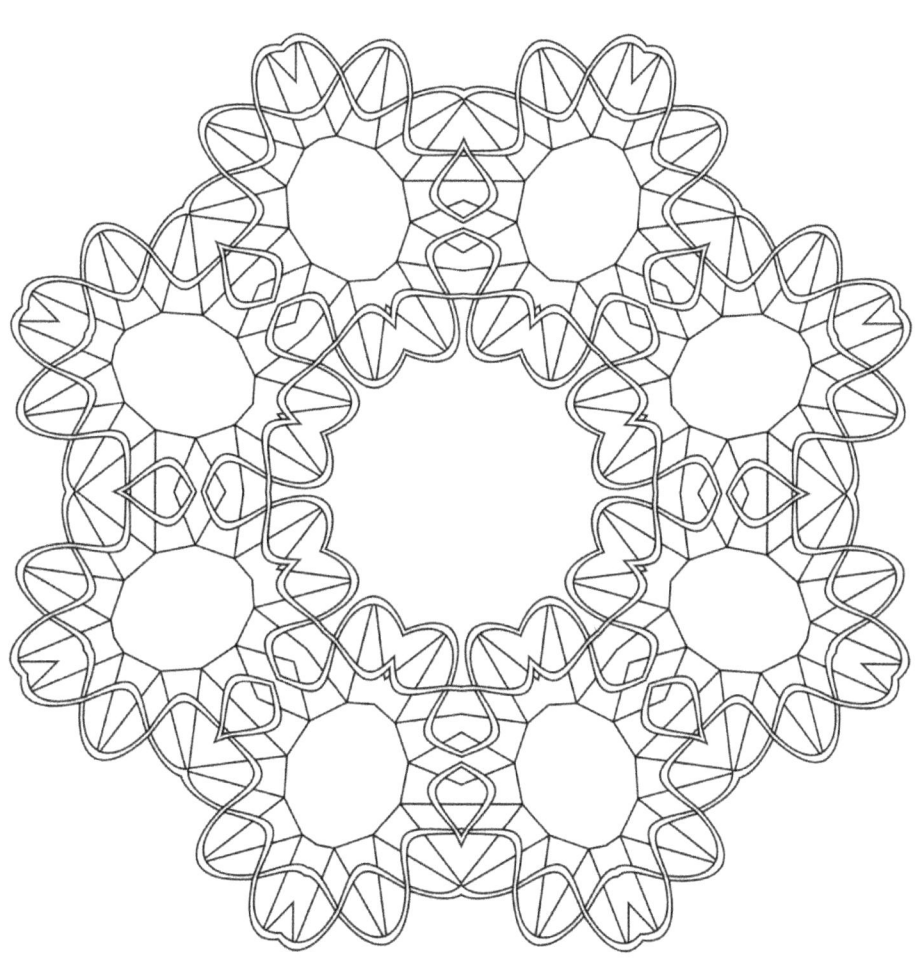

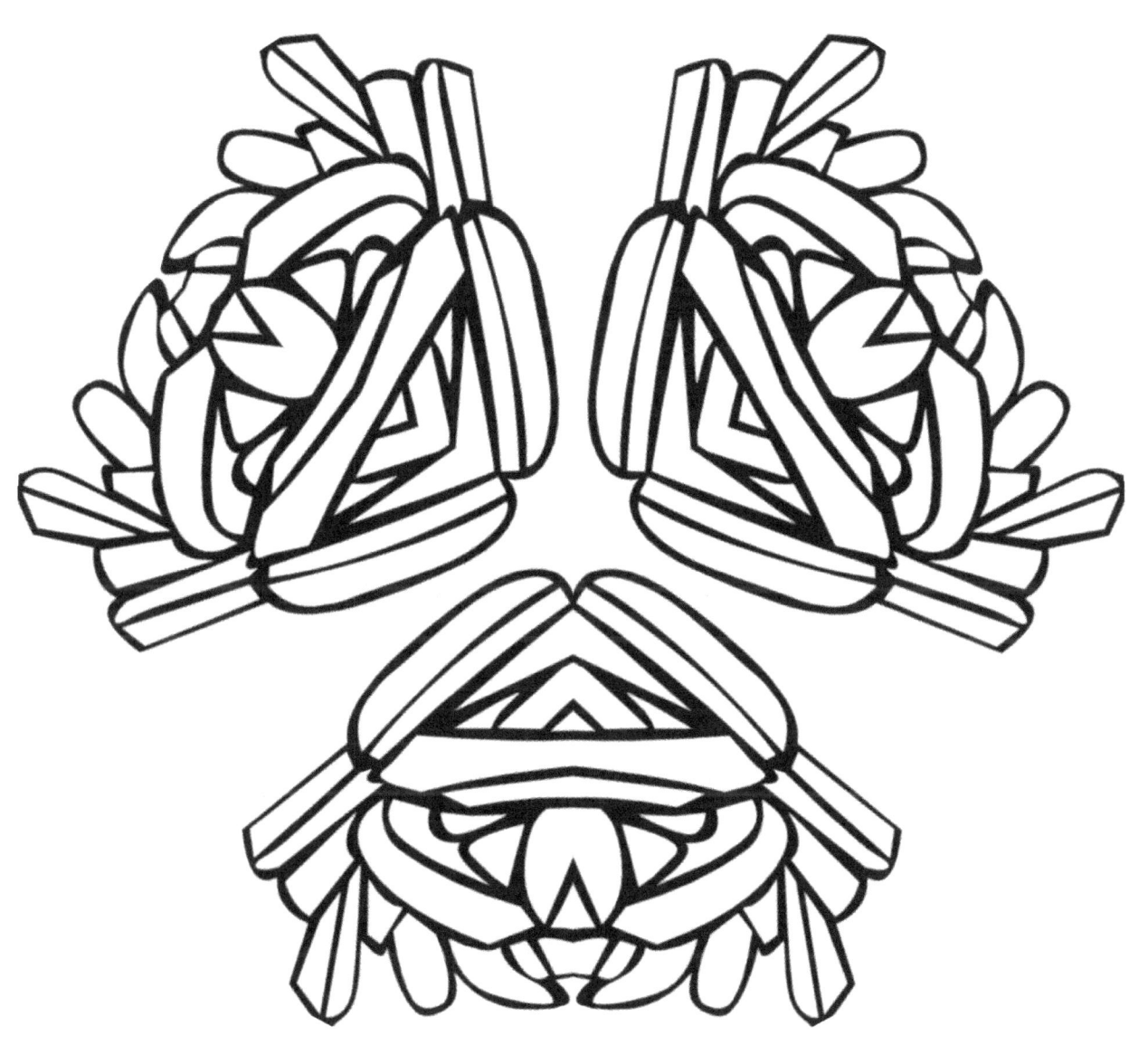

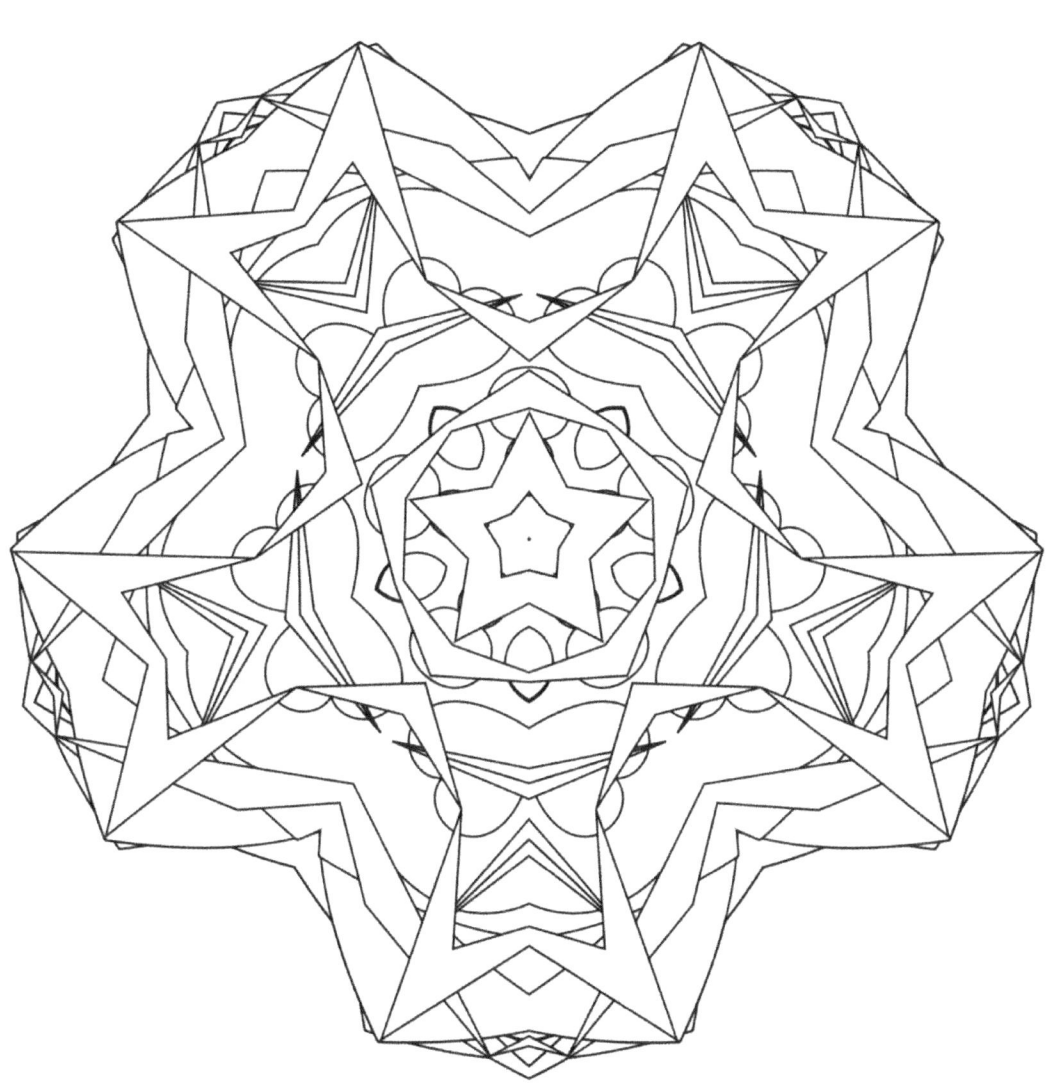

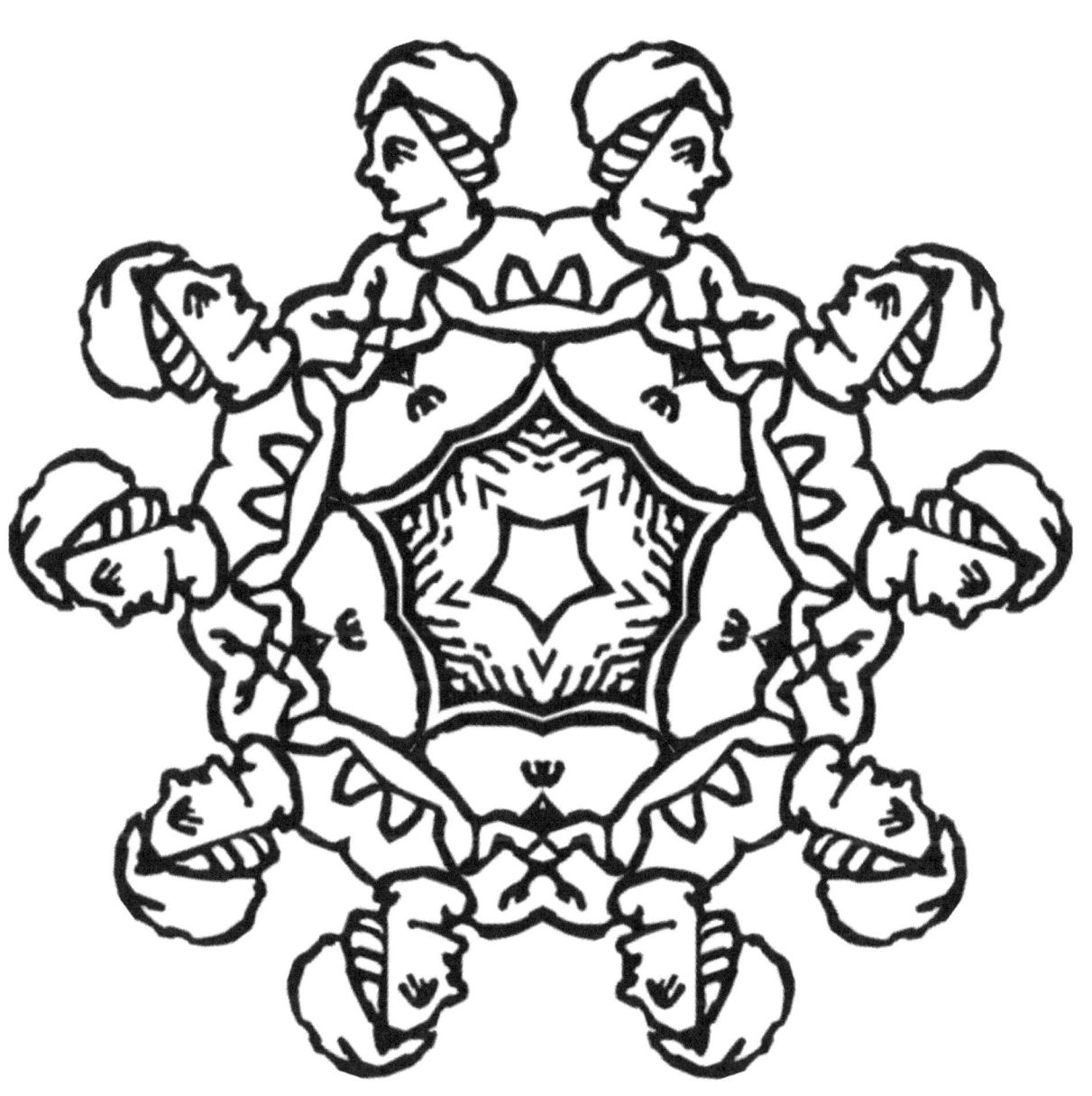

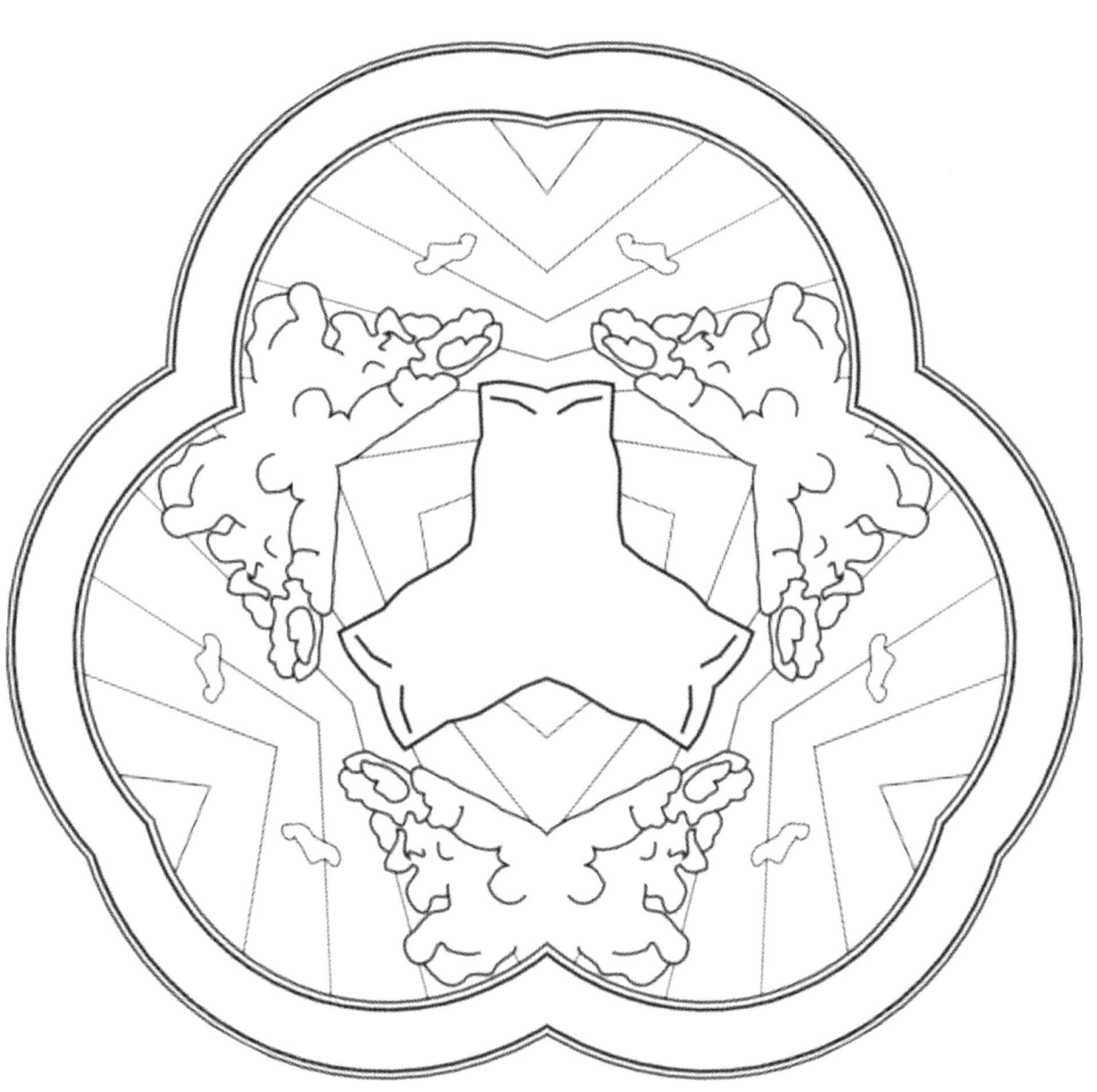

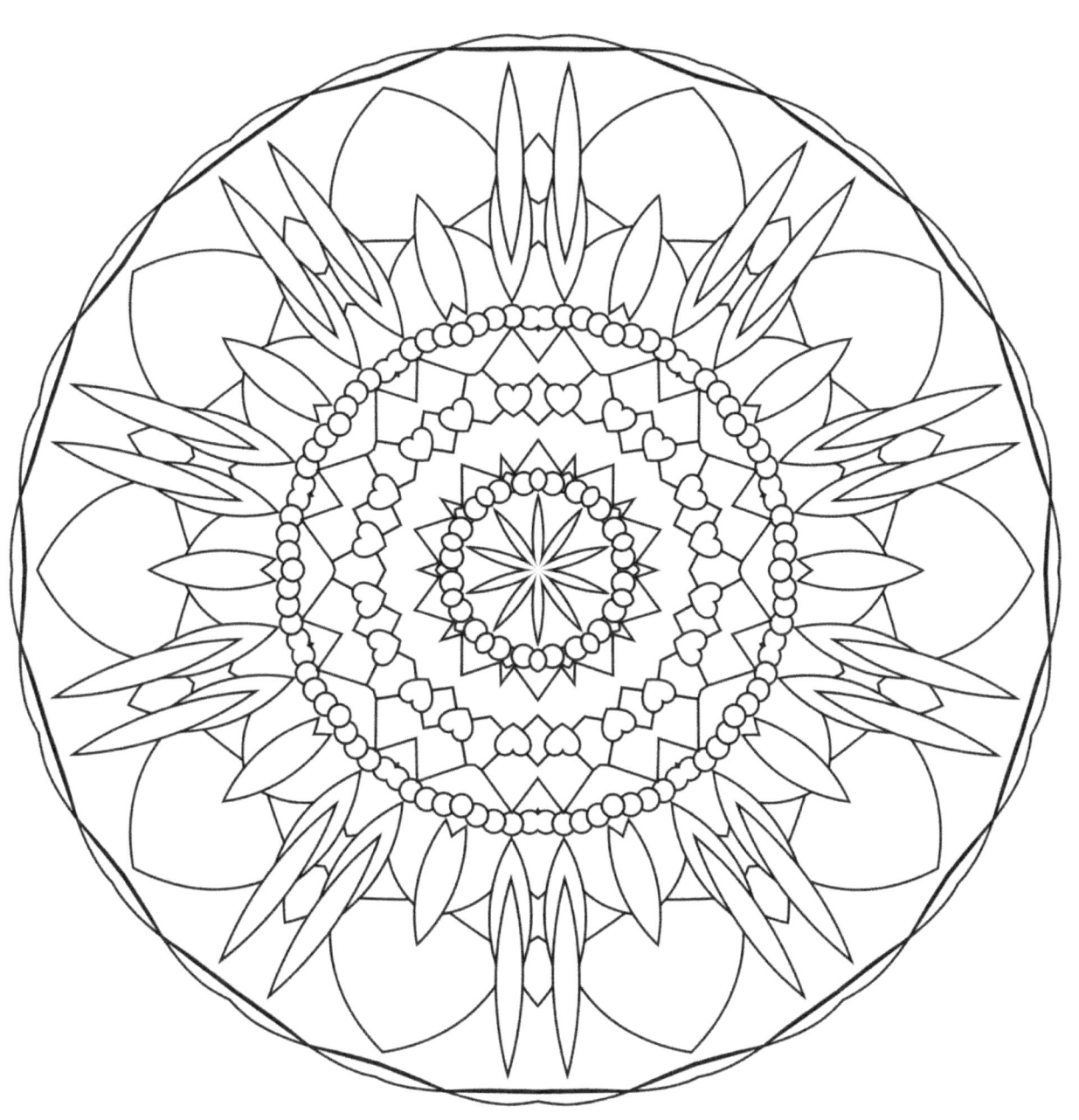

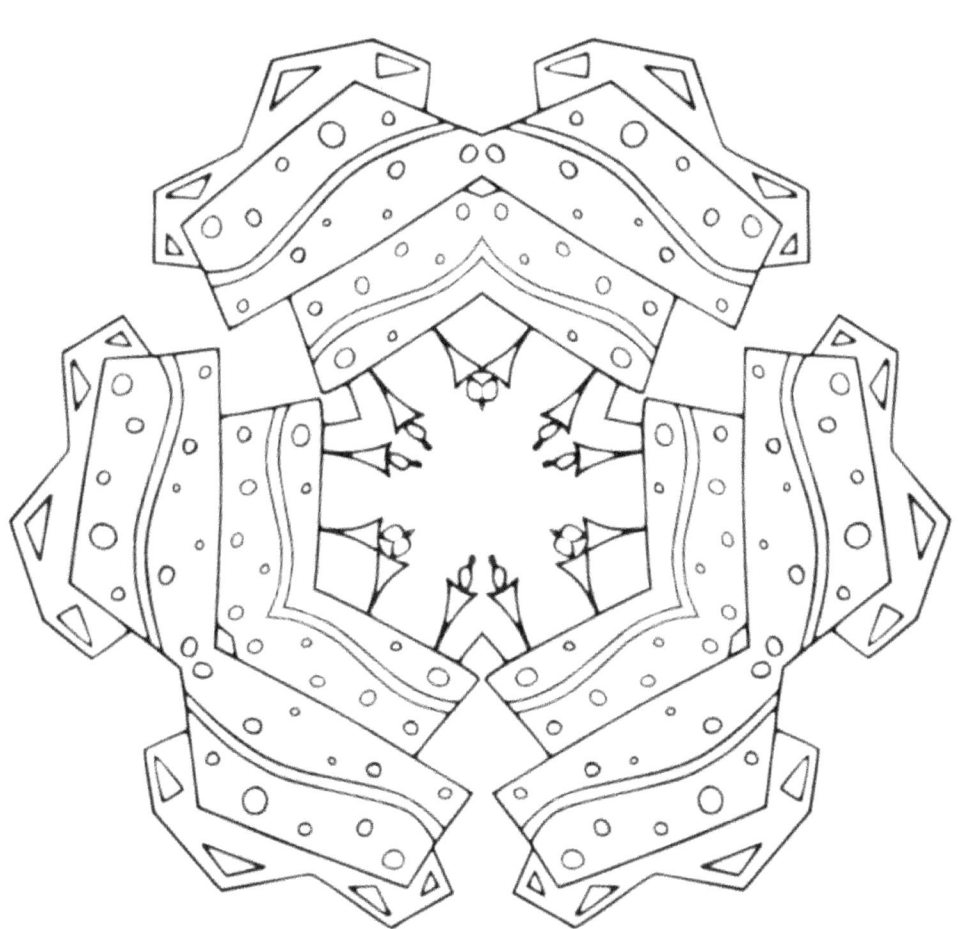

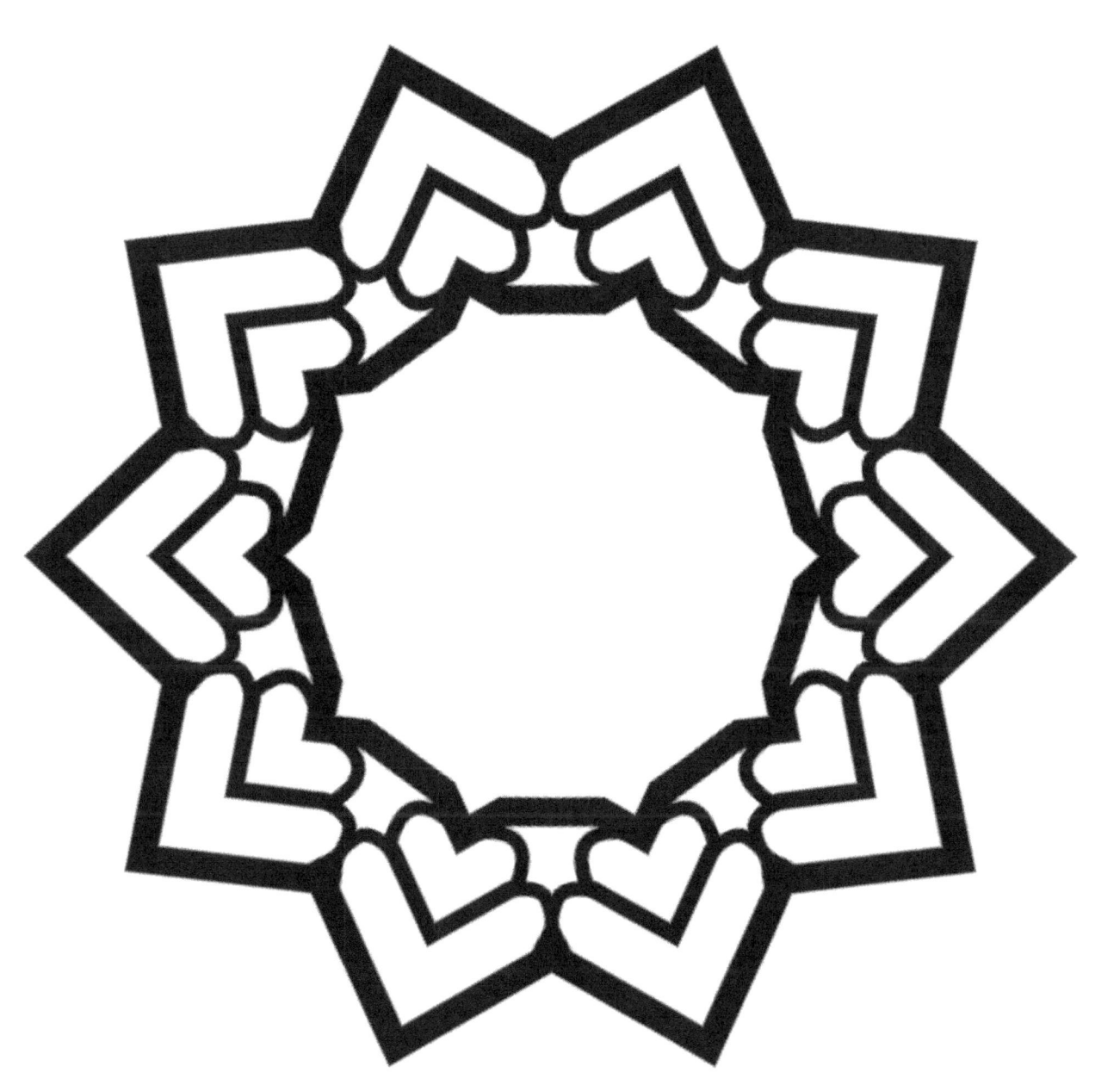

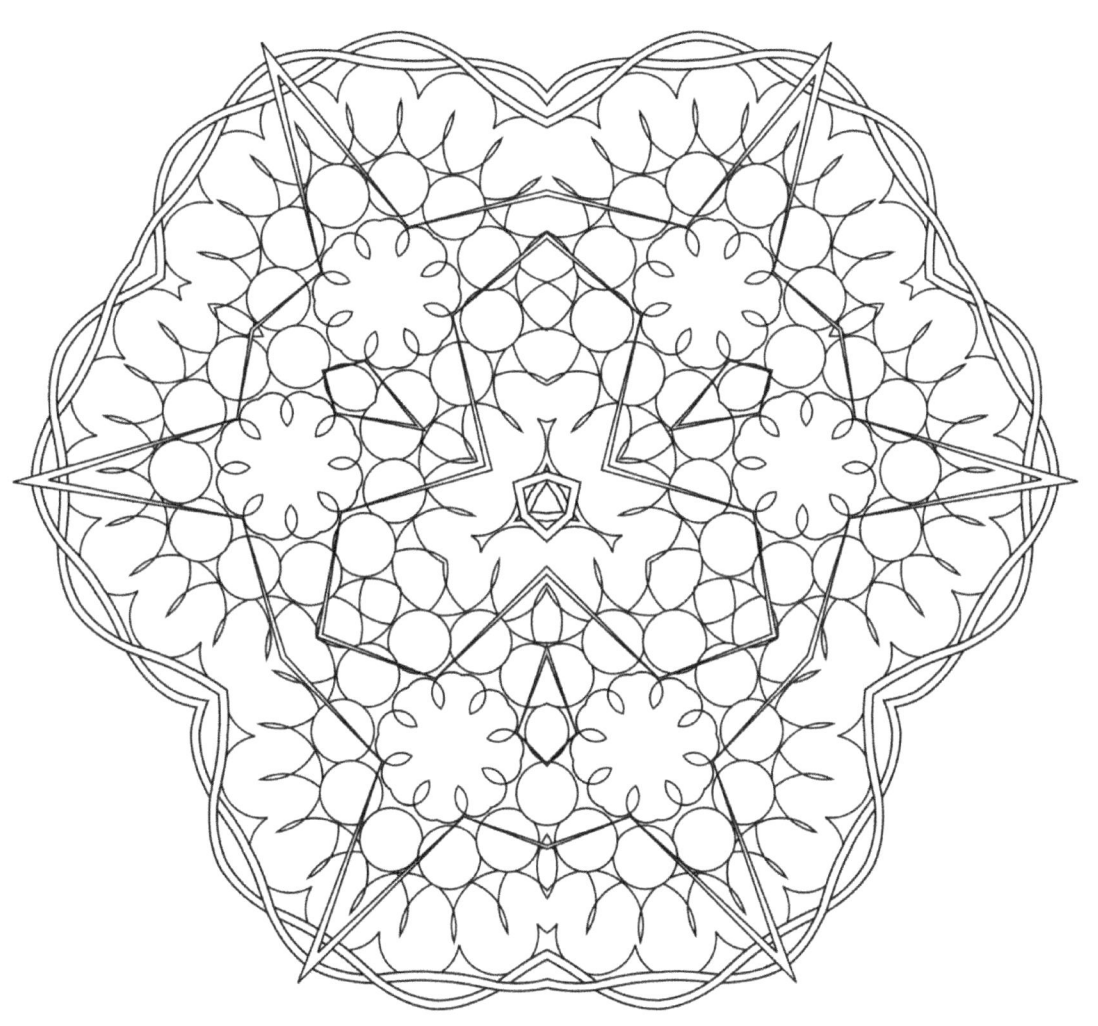

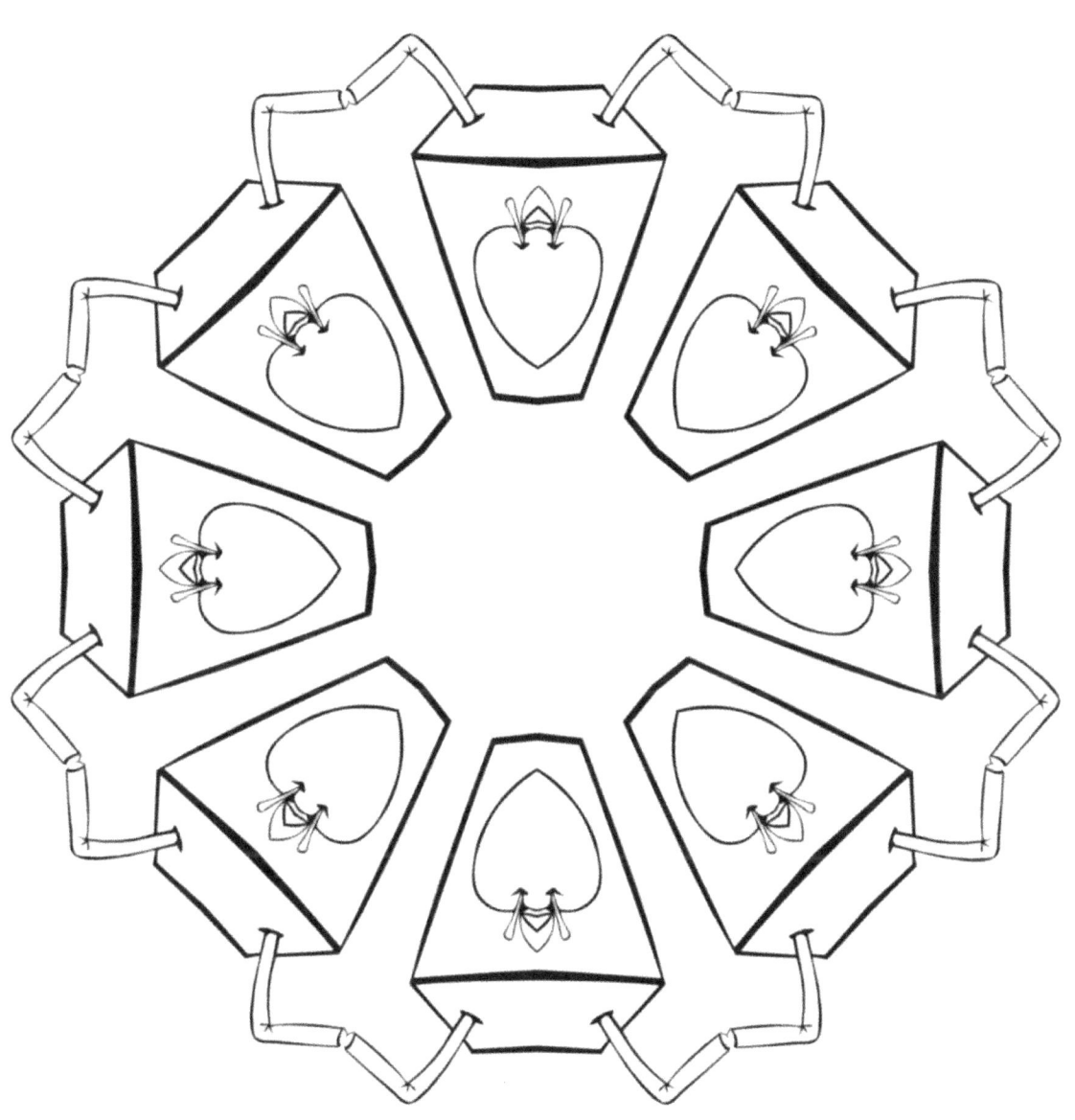

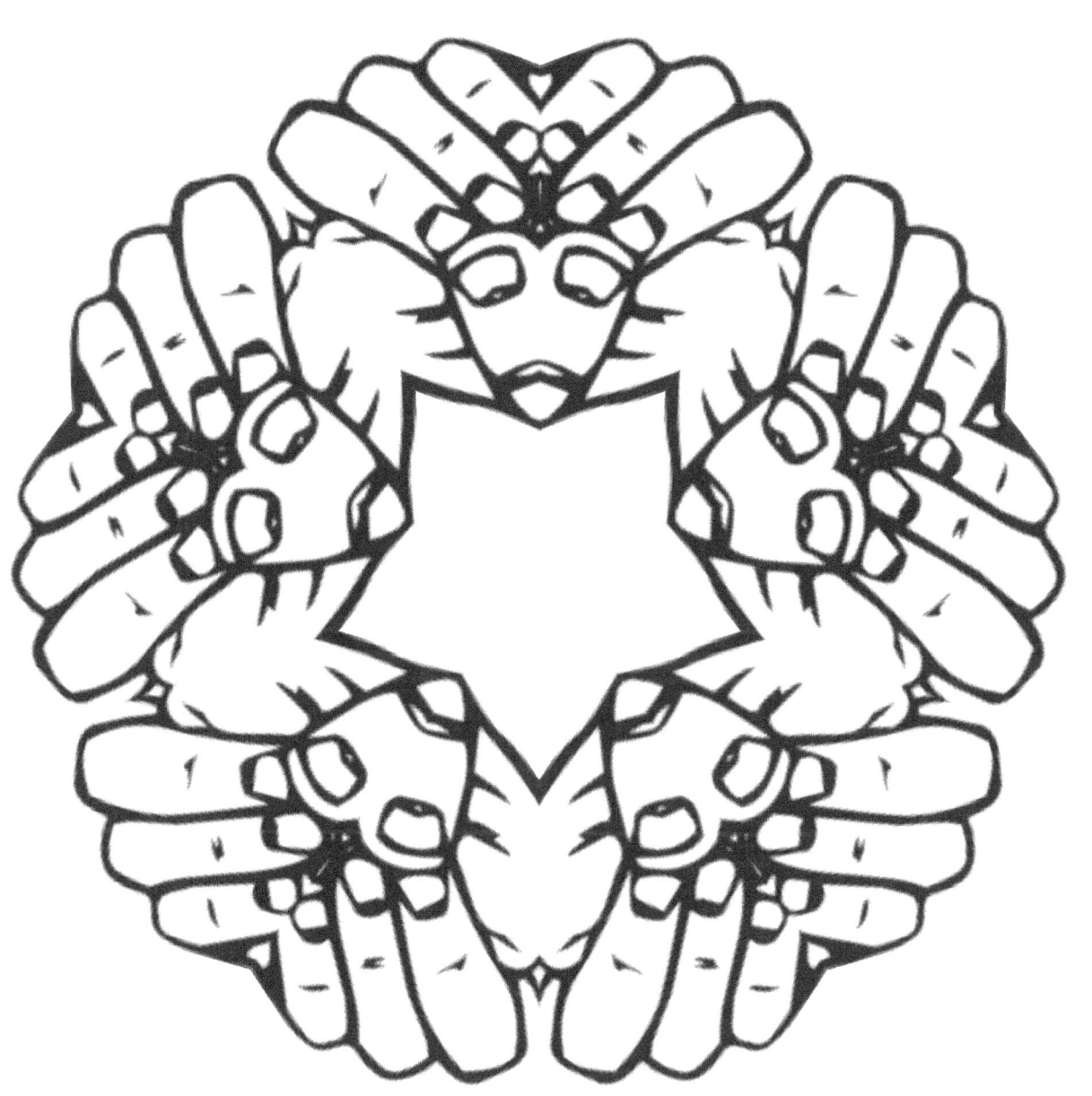

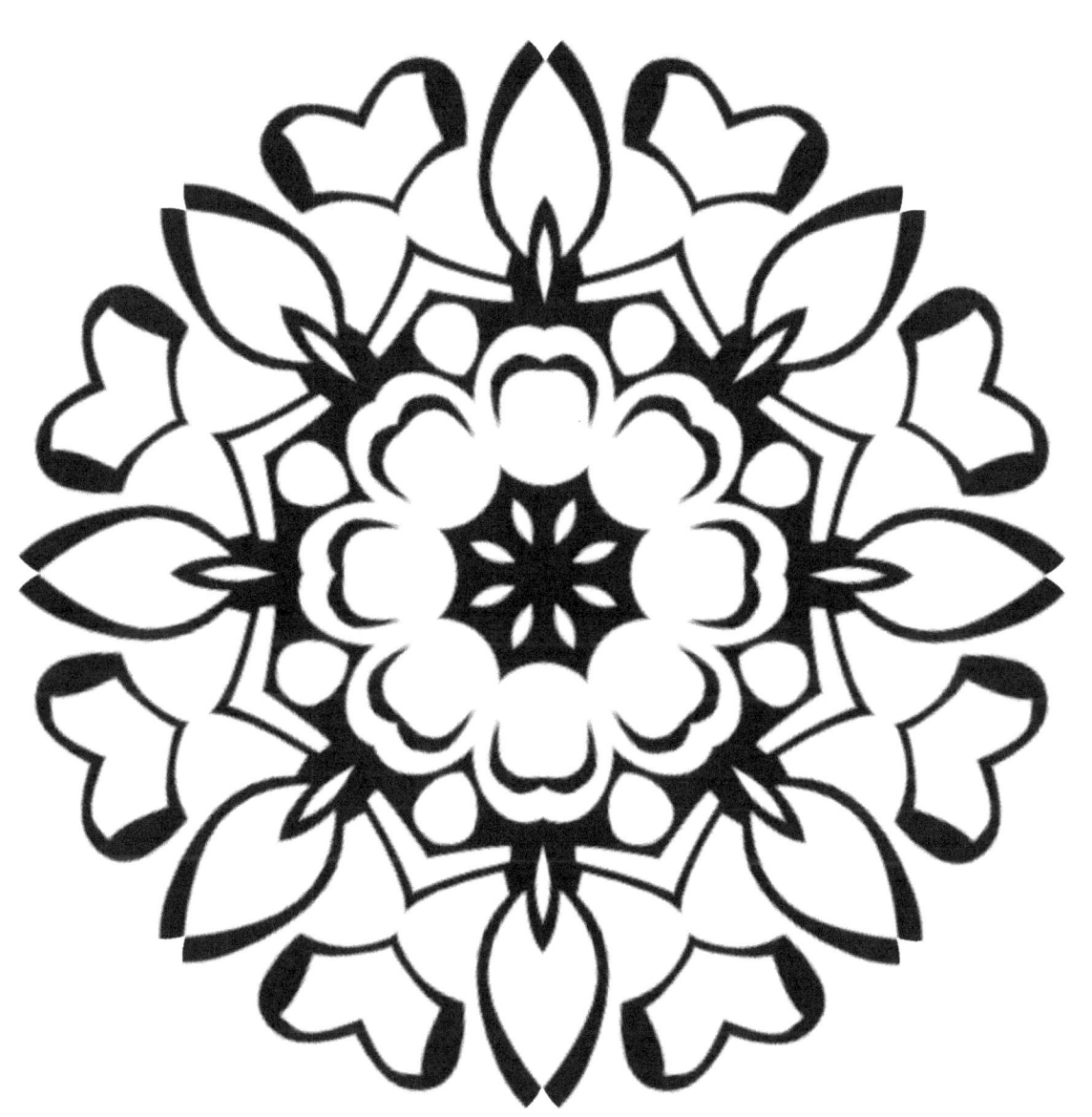

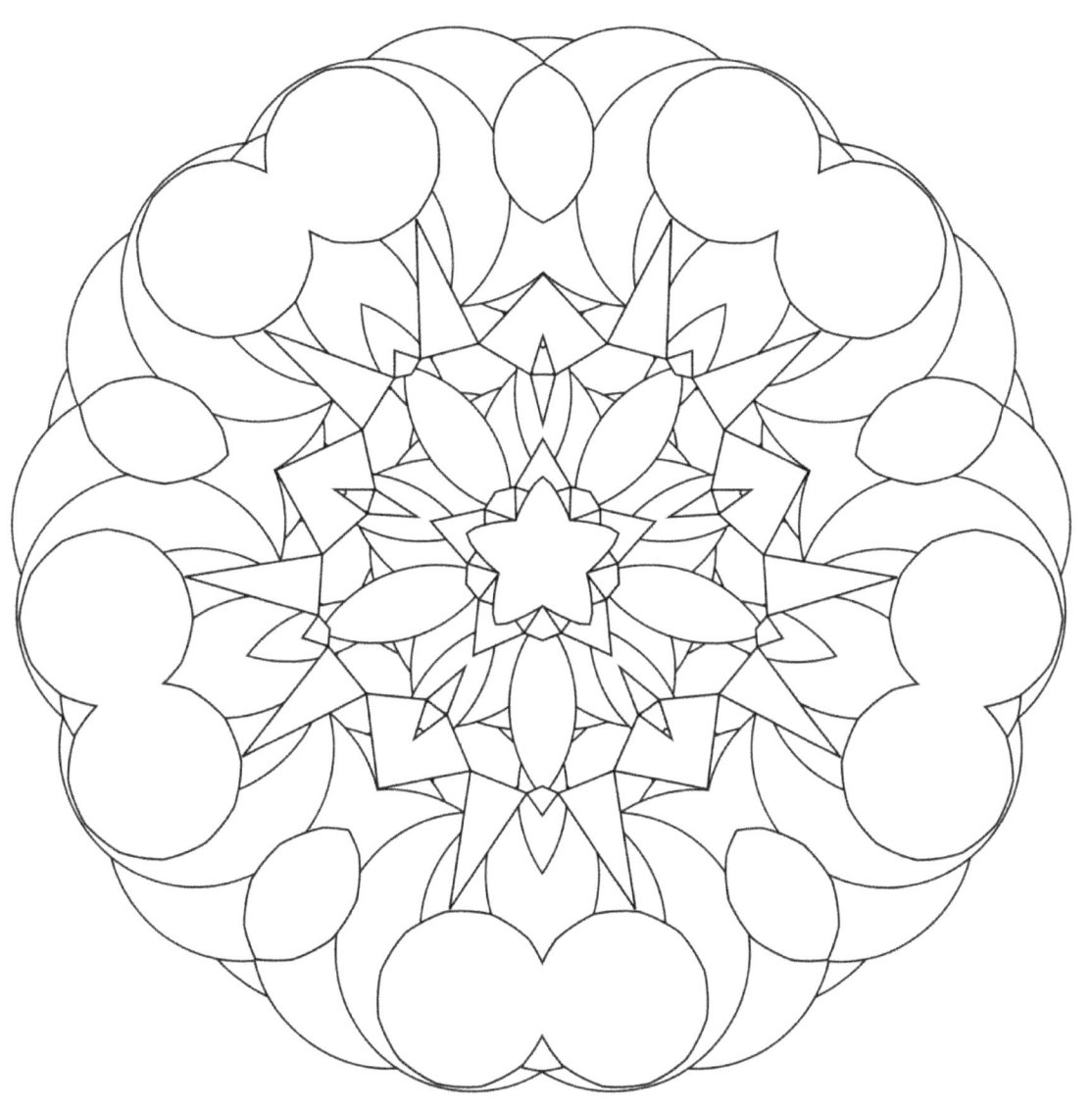

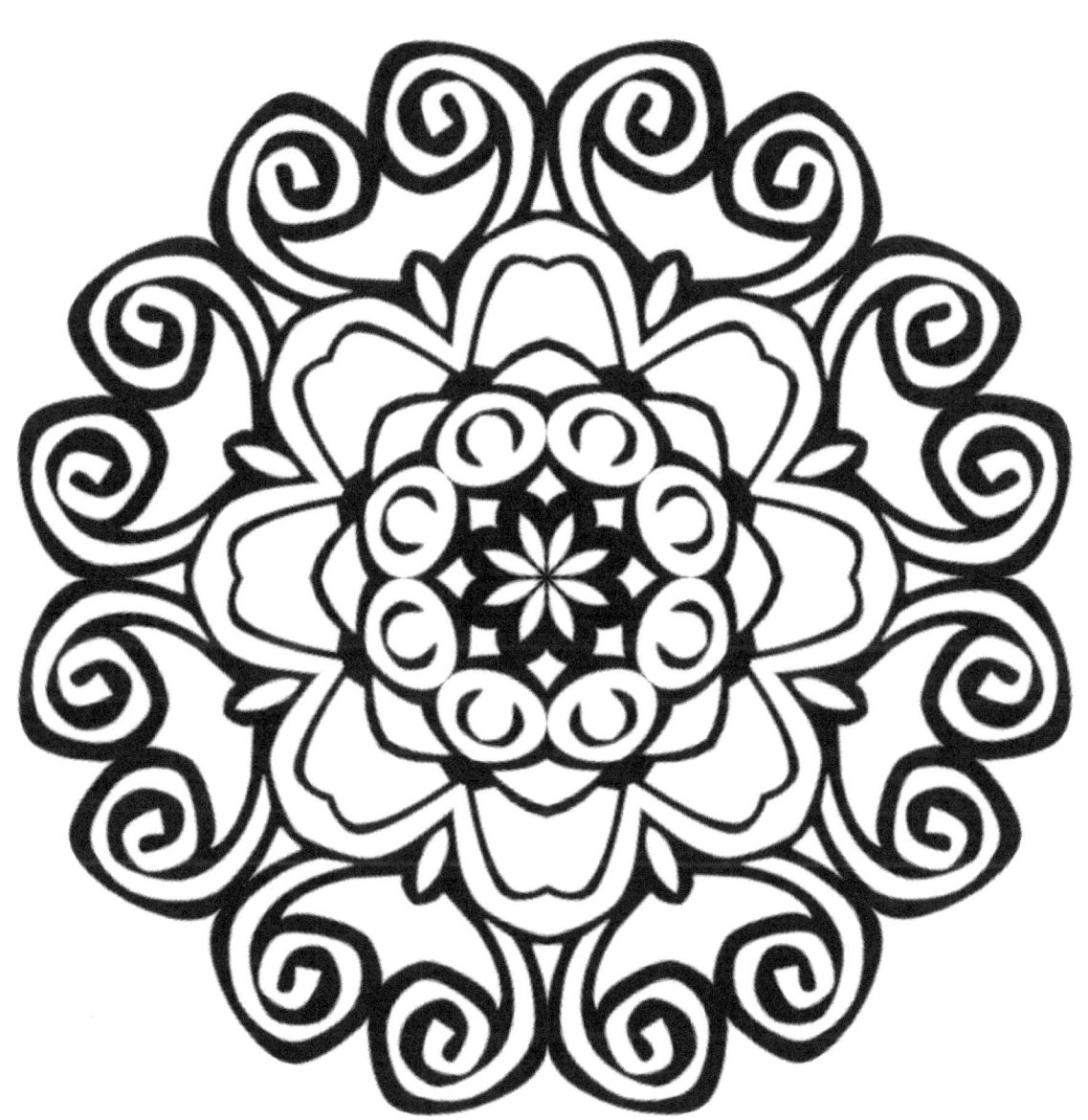

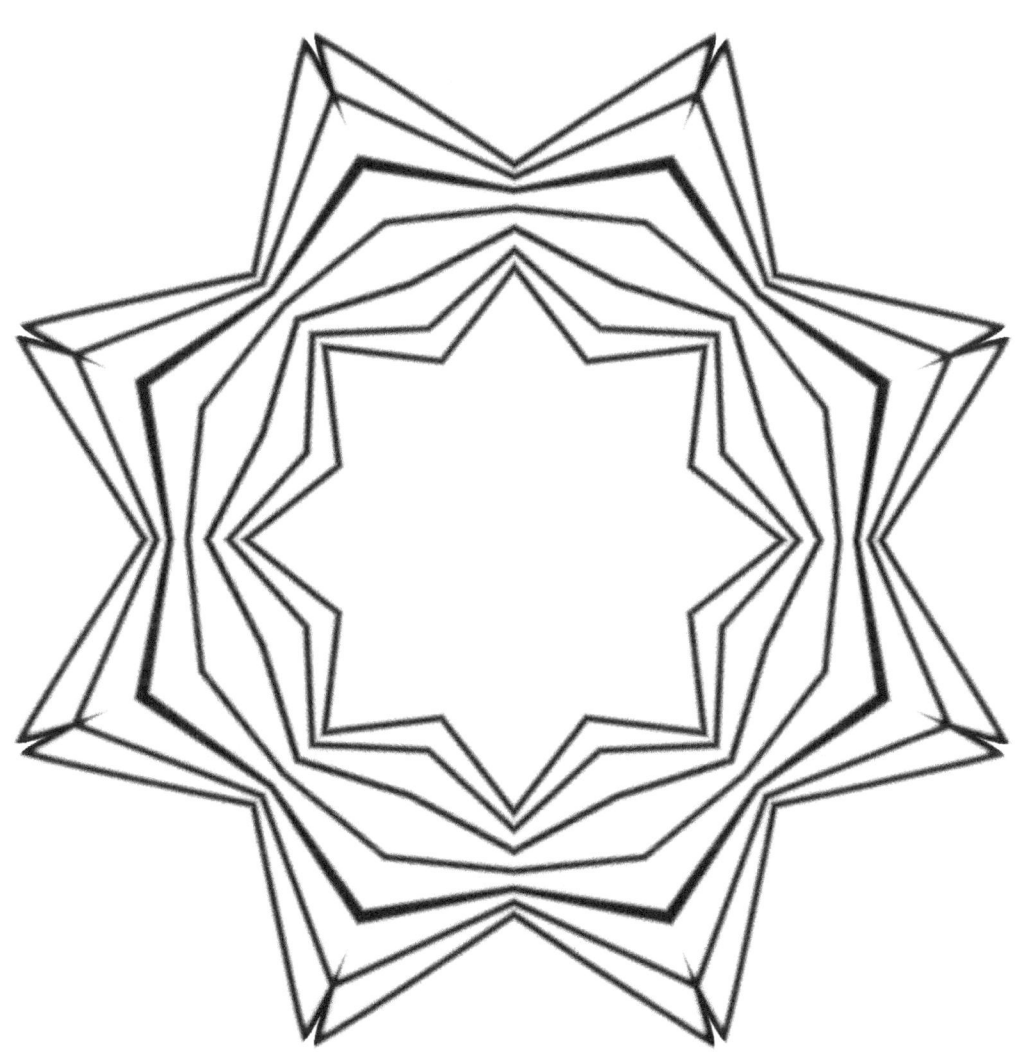

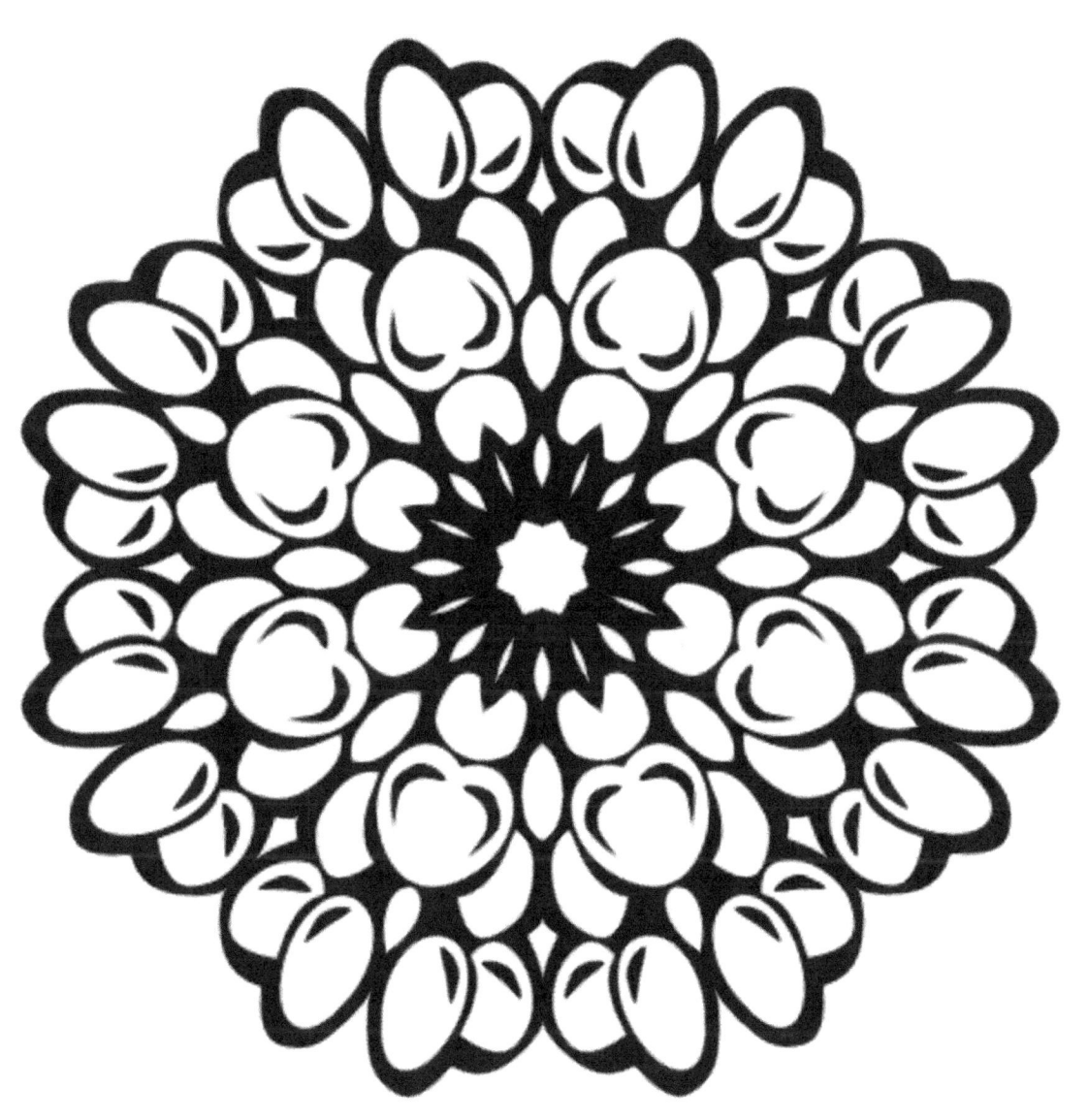

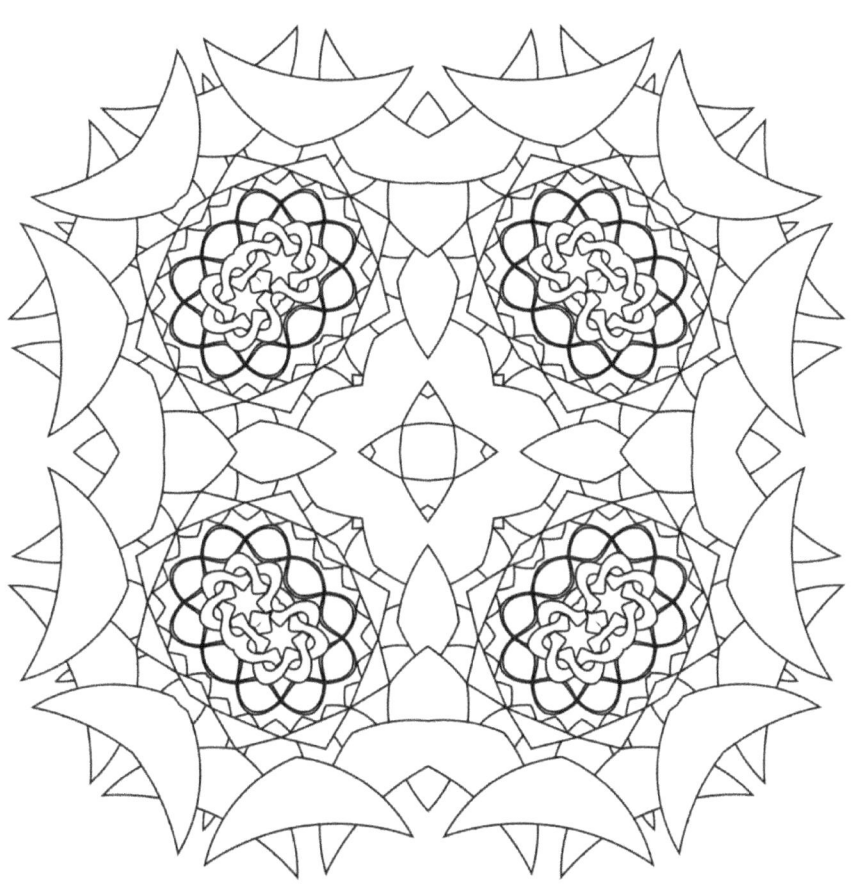

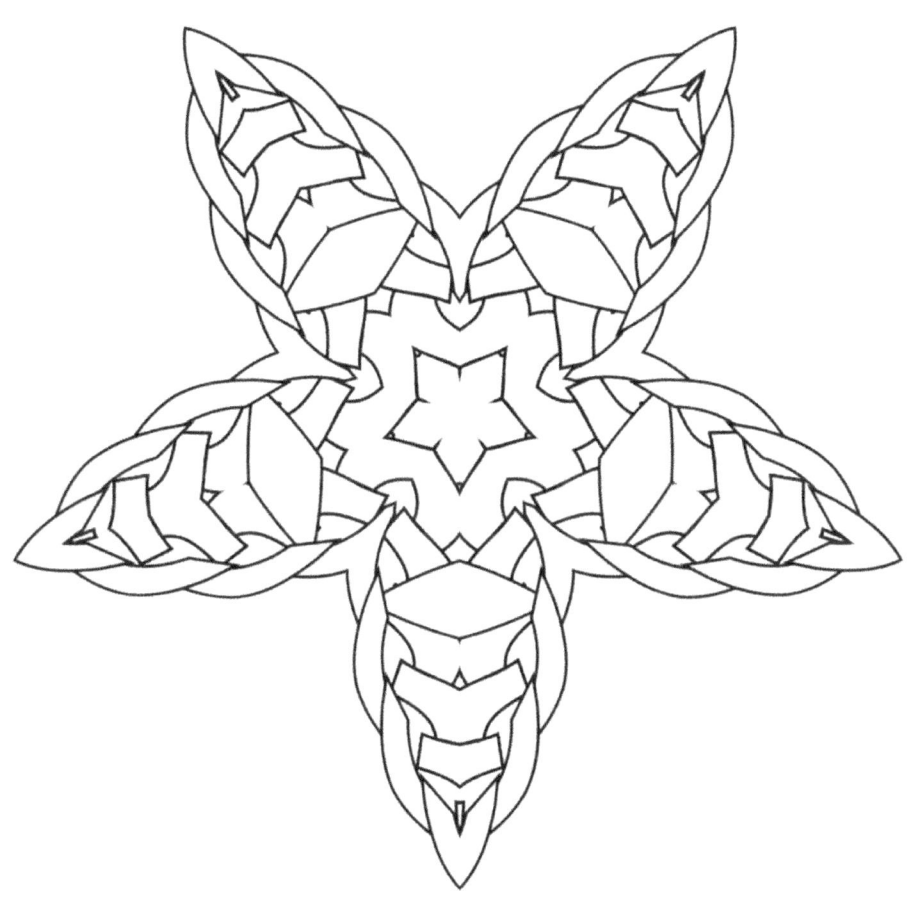

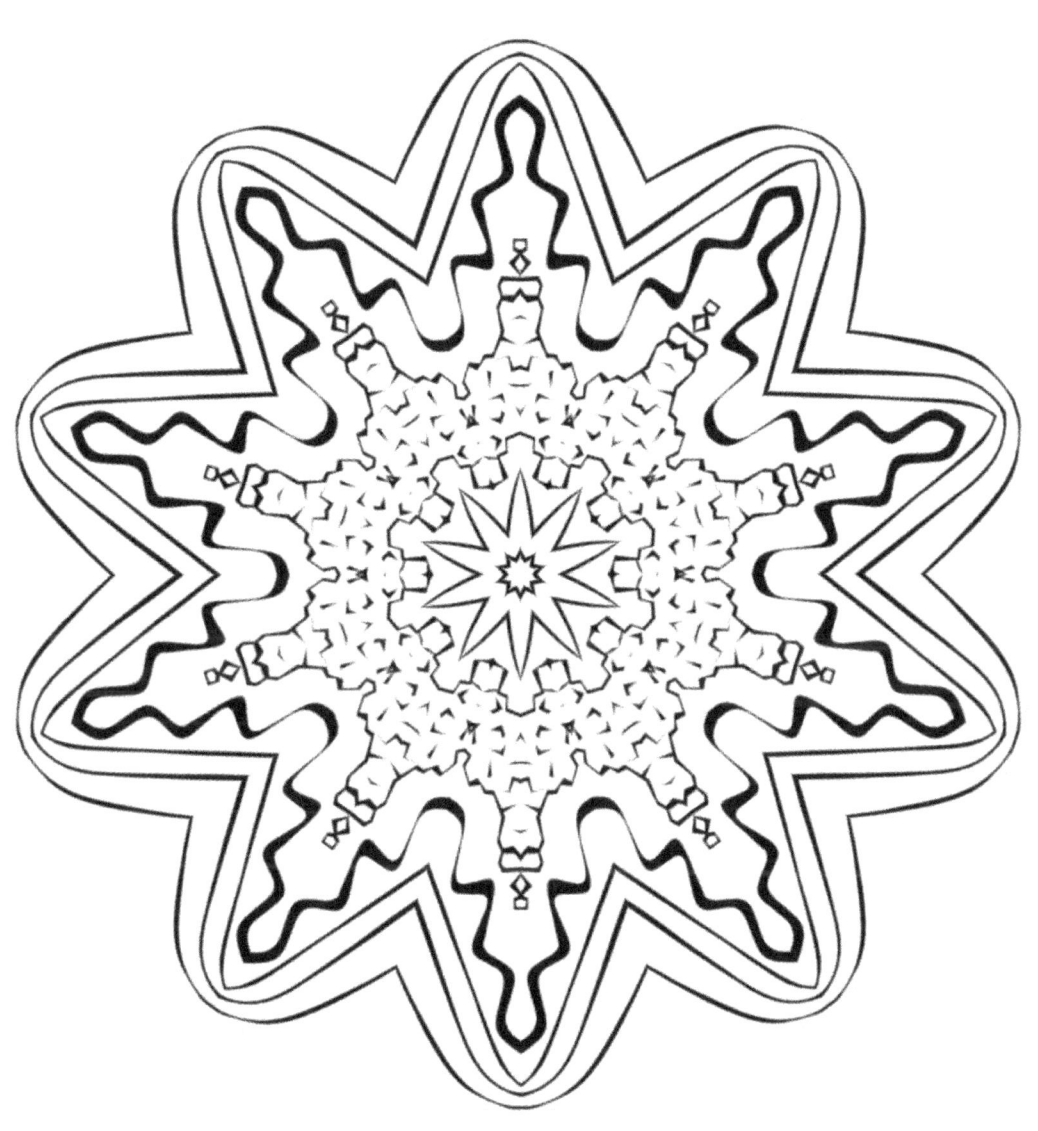

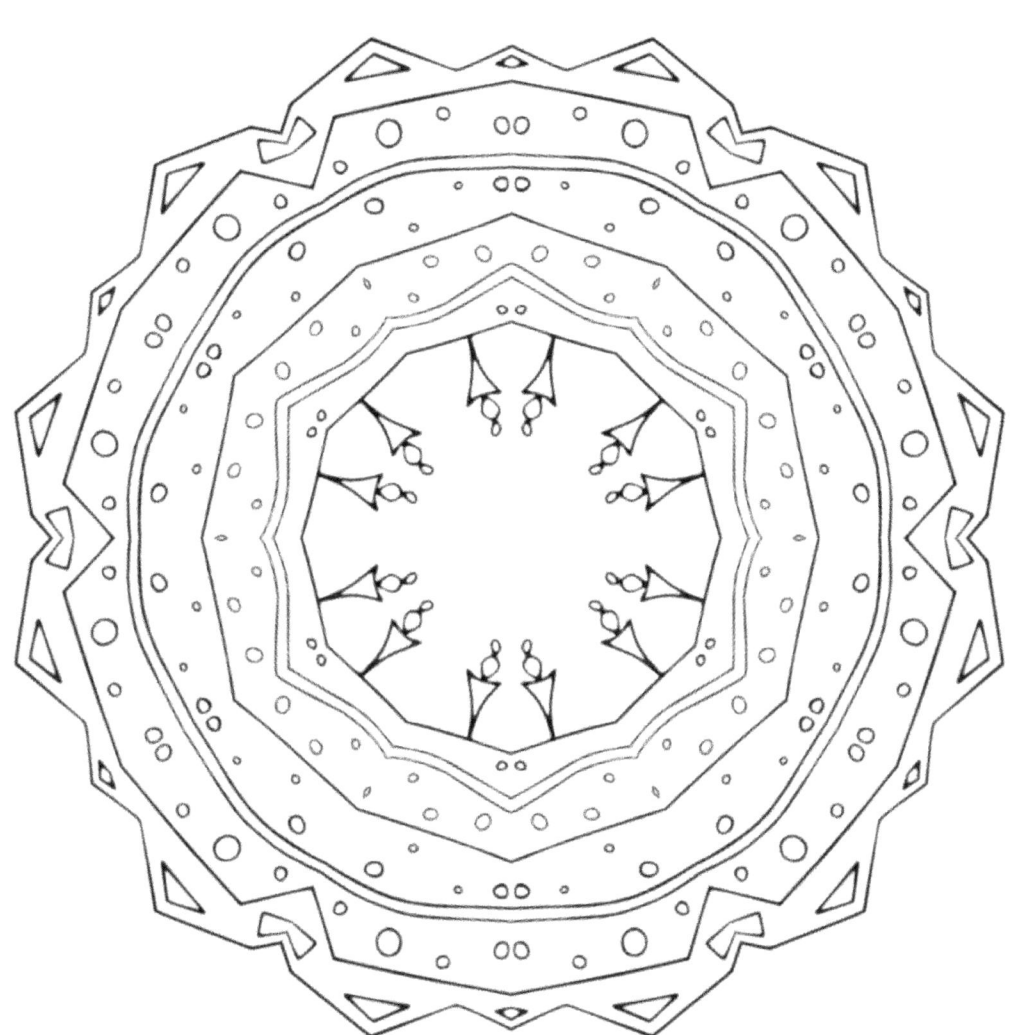

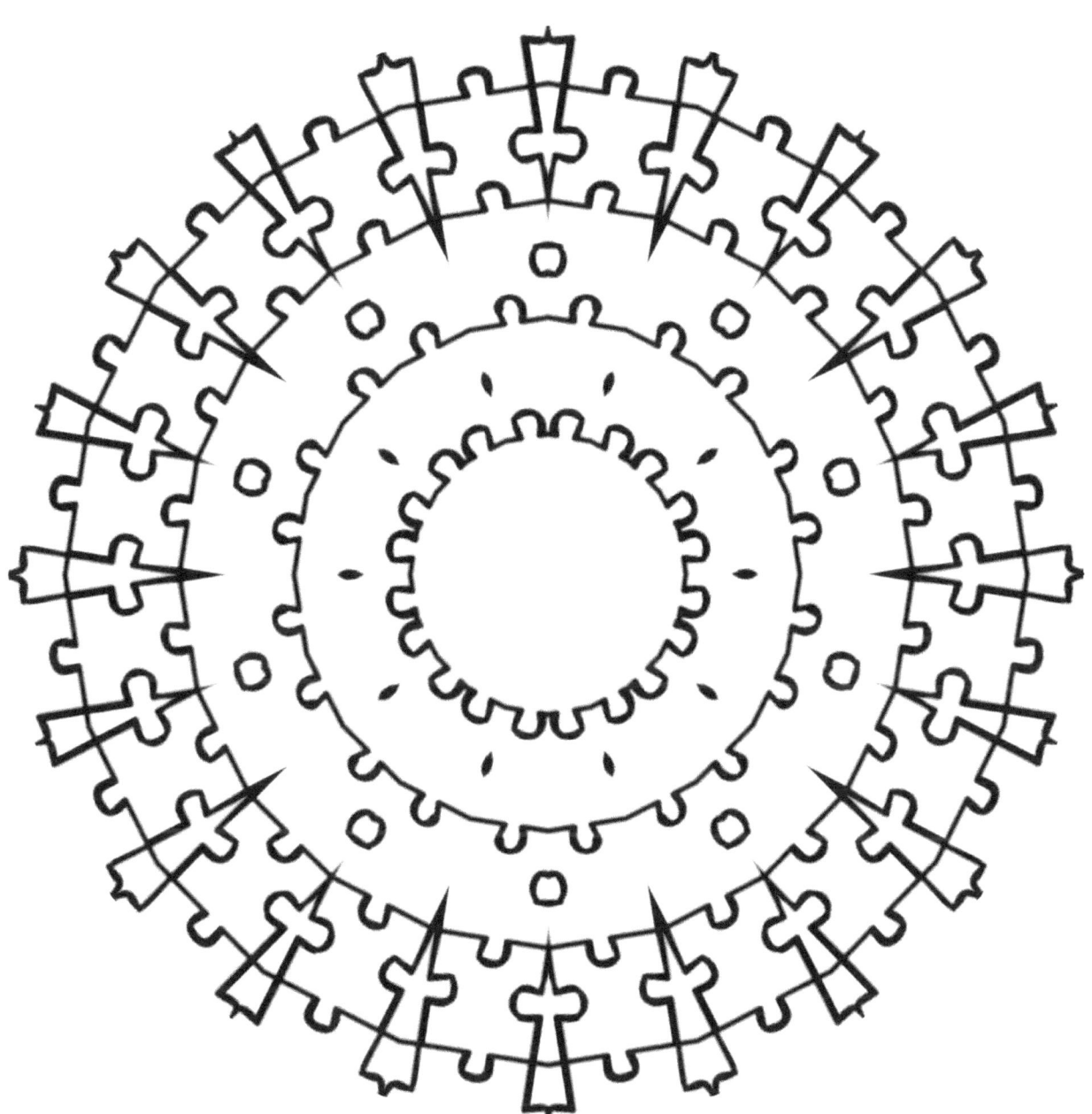

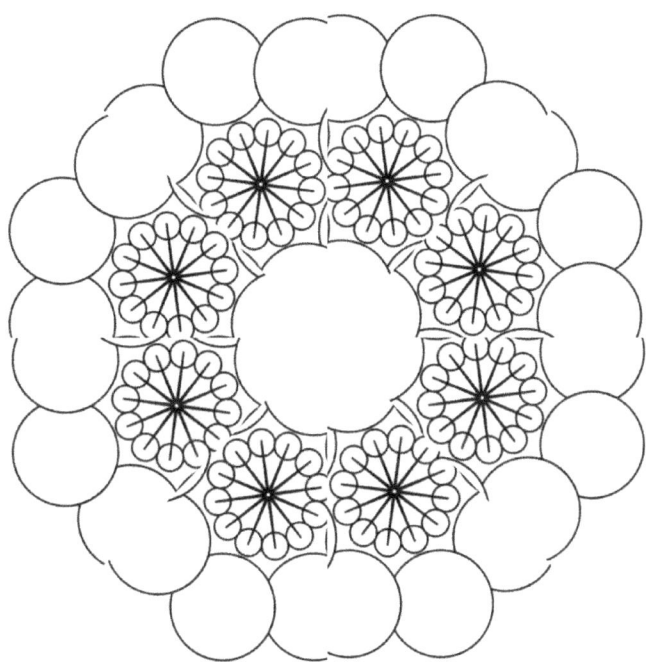

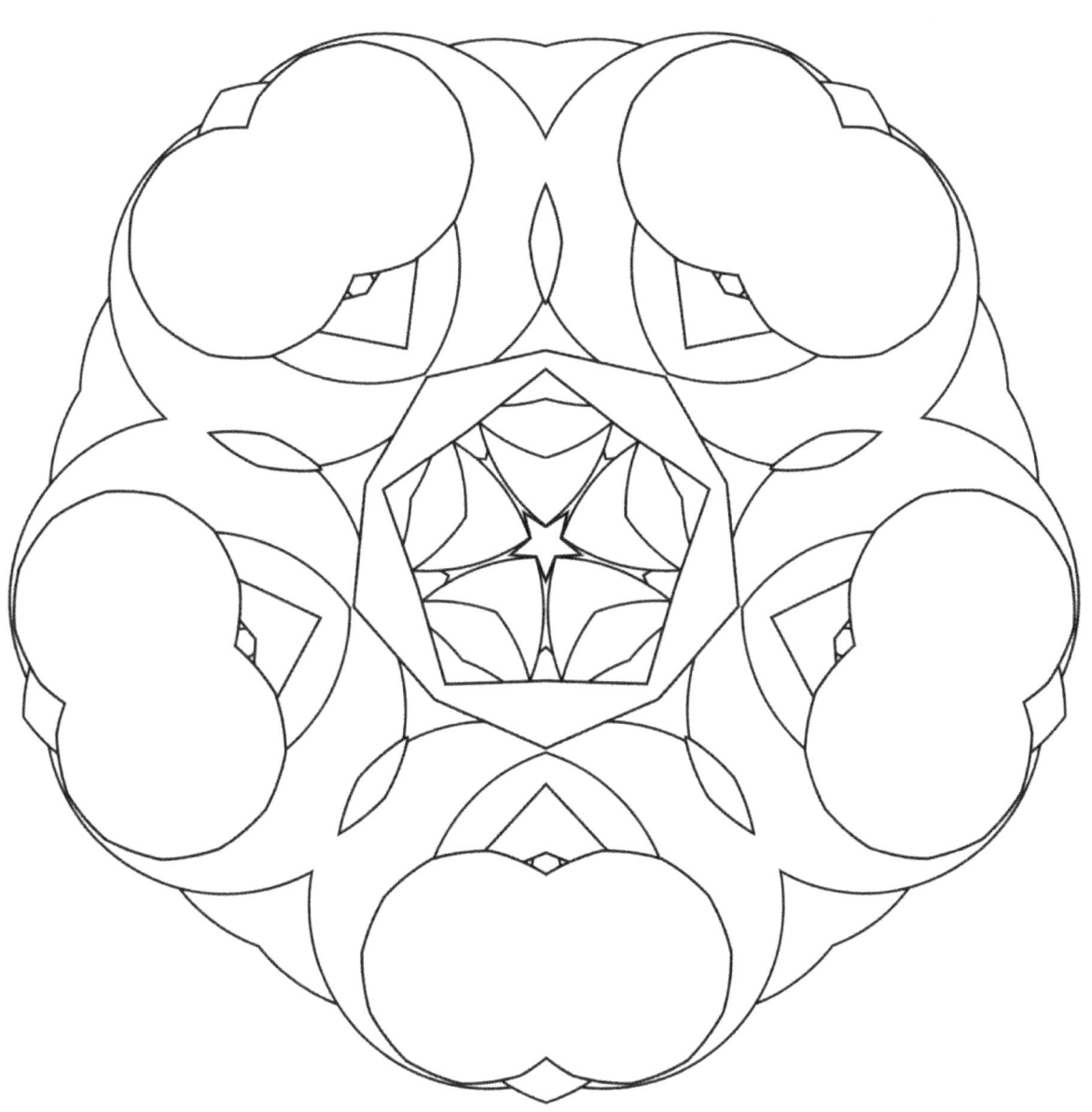

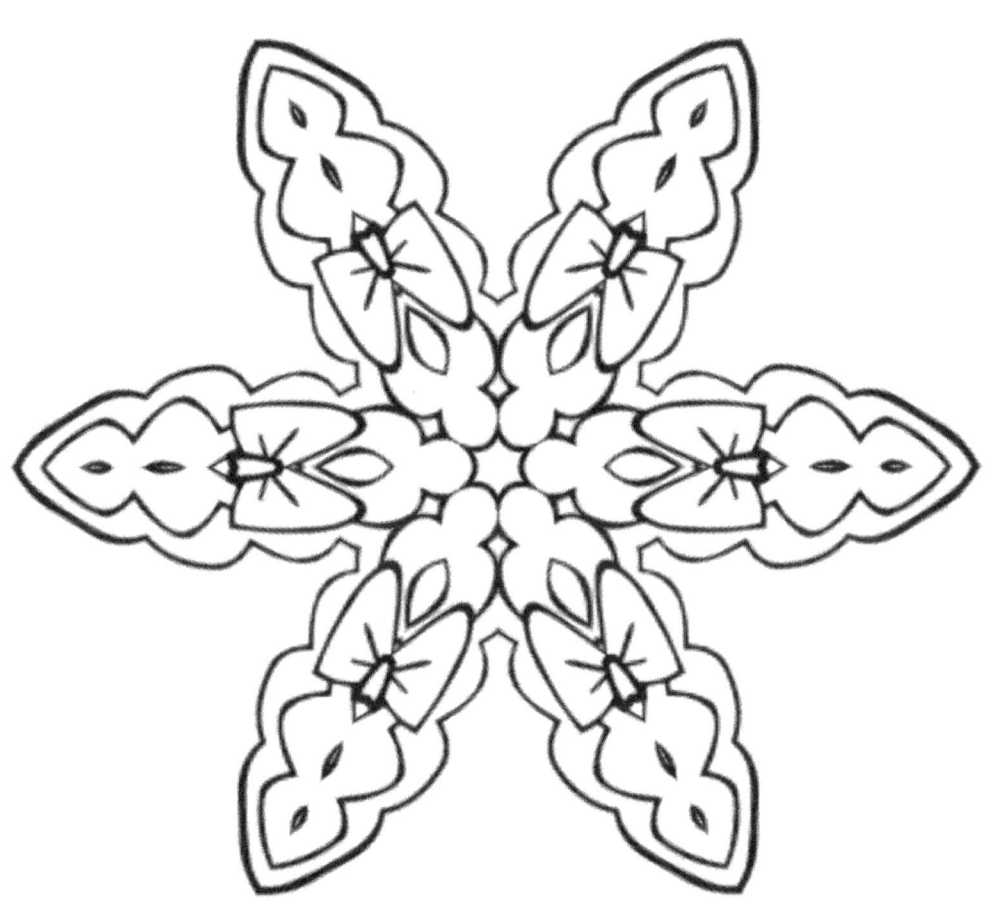

Thank you for purchasing Volume 1 of the Kaleidoscope Series. I hope you have enjoyed coloring the kaleidoscopes as much as I did designing them.

I also want to thank my dear husband, John Hogan, for his never ending support.

Please look for Volume 2 of the Kaleidoscope Series coming out soon as well as Volume 1 of the Zirkel Series and Stoner Series.

Email: <u>favoritesofruthies@gmail.com</u>